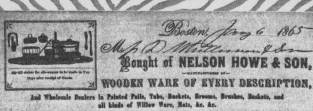

Boston, *Jany 6* 1865

M͟ₛ D Whitm... & Son

Bought of **NELSON HOWE & SON,**

— MANUFACTURER OF —

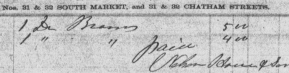

WOODEN WARE OF EVERY DESCRIPTION,

And Wholesale Dealers in Painted Pails, Tubs, Buckets, Brooms, Brushes, Baskets, and all kinds of Willow Ware, Mats, &c. &c.

Nos. 31 & 32 SOUTH MARKET, and 31 & 32 CHATHAM STREETS.

1 Dz Brooms		5 00
1 " "	Paid	4 00

Nelson Howe & Son

Boston, *May 15* 1841

M Guy T Grouse

Bought of ROBERT STEELE,

J. Howe, Printer.]

Dealer in Wooden Ware, Rattans, Mats, Brooms, Cane Poles, &c. Wholesale and Retail,

No. 26, Dock Square,

1 Dz Rake			3 00
1½ Dz "			2 37
½ Dz Sift Scutt	9ac		4 50
1 half Bushel			37
3 Store orch	5 00		15 0
2 Mats			3 3
1 Dz Pails			2 25
1 Shovel Handle	12		$14 39
Recd Payt R Steele			14 44
Thos O Tappan			

EARLY AMERICAN WOODEN WARE

EARLY
AMERICAN
WOODEN WARE

& Other Kitchen Utensils

by Mary Earle Gould

CHARLES E. TUTTLE CO., INC.
RUTLAND, VERMONT

Representatives
Continental Europe: BOXERBOOKS, INC., *Zurich*
British Isles: PRENTICE-HALL INTERNATIONAL, INC., *London*
Australasia : BOOK WISE (AUSTRALIA) PTY. LTD.
104-108 Sussex Street, Sydney 2000

Published by the Charles E. Tuttle Company, Inc.
of Rutland, Vermont & Tokyo, Japan
with editorial offices at Suido 1-chome, 2-6
Bunkyo-ku, Tokyo, Japan

Library of Congress Catalog Card No. 69-13499

International Standard Book No. 0-8048-0153-3

Fifth printing, 1979

PRINTED IN JAPAN

DEDICATION

In the years following the first appearance of EARLY AMERICAN WOODEN WARE many of my friends who helped me have passed away. From them I had both inspiration and assistance. It is fitting, therefore, that this new edition be dedicated to the memory of Clara Endicott Sears, William Sumner Appleton, George Francis Dow, Charles Messer Stow, Lewis N. Wiggins, William B. Sprague, Frank K. Swain, my "great-grandmother" Mrs. Worth, and Hugh Thatcher, the cooper, from England. And to these loyal helpers I must add the name of my mother, Mrs. John W. Gould (1855-1959) who was my greatest inspiration and critic — who tolerated my mistakes and gave me faith in myself.

Plate 1. 200-year-old Elm Tree in Old Deerfield, Massachusetts, showing some of its many burls.

THE CONTENTS

CONTENTS — Continued

ILLUSTRATIONS

"The Wooden Ware Room" . . . part of the author's
  private museum

ILLUSTRATIONS—*Continued*

XI

ILLUSTRATIONS—*Continued*

FOREWORD

STANDING before my museum of wooden ware, num-bering nearly eight hundred pieces and including a pantry box collection, one's first impulse is to ask how it happened. Things can happen with no deliberate intent, and this "happening" of mine came merely as a hobby. It came at a time when my days were full with the profession of music — teaching, playing and lecturing.

In the fall of 1932 I found an old cheese box in a shed "up country." I was antiquing with a collector friend and had expressed no interest or enthusiasm for any of the so-called antiques. However, this article appealed to me as a

Plate 2. The first box of the collection with a view of the bottom and the small oval box that was the second find.

container for my rag-rug pieces. It took a second trip to buy the box as the owner was reluctant to let it go.

I had the box scraped and shellacked but fortunately left intact the owner's name, lettered in yellow on the bottom, "S. Reed," who at one time lived in the childhood home of my father. A chance second box an oval spice box, gave me the impetus to ask for boxes as I drove about and visited antique shops. Not knowing anything about such boxes I expected to be enlightened by dealers and by books in libraries. But dealers at that time knew nothing about them and cared less, considering them such common articles as to be of no account; and libraries in my own and several distant cities had no references to boxes, and not even a picture could be uncovered.

Within six months my collection numbered twenty-seven boxes and they were all different. My curiosity was aroused and I found myself studying the shapes, analyzing any odor and examining the workmanship. I drew my own conclusions as to what each box had once held. The round shape of the cheese box and of the butter box, the odors of spices and the stains of salaratus, the mark of the sugar scoop, and the size of the herb and the pill boxes — all helped me to figure out the original uses for which the boxes were made.

My inherent gift of writing urged me to pen the story of my collection. I wanted to set down my discoveries and strengthen my own deductions. I went to auctions, visited any and all shops within reasonable distance and even went into private homes when an invitation had been given.

Like any new plaything, the boxes were a keen joy to me and I wanted to show them to my friends. One day I started out in my car to see a friend, taking with me my choicest boxes. I stopped at Northampton, Massachusetts, where Wiggins Tavern has made its name both as a hotel and as a museum. While I sat at luncheon, Mr. Lewis Wiggins, in the role of host, spoke to me and, as one collector to another, I told him of my box collection. Mr. Wiggins asked to see the boxes in my car and soon we were comparing them with those of his own collection. We discussed every angle of those pantry receptacles. Mr. Wiggins expressed the desire that I write an article for his friend, Mr. Charles Messer Stow of the *New York Sun*. That article appeared in the Saturday antique section in the spring of 1934, the first of a group that followed. I do not recall whether or not I continued on the way to see my friend that day!

Still not satisfied with the little I knew about boxes, I wrote to Clara Endicott Sears of Harvard, Massachusetts. Miss Sears is an authority on the history of Shaker indus-tries, having established Fruitlands, of Bronson Alcott fame. Miss Sears sent me to William Sumner Appleton of Boston, organizer of the Society for the Preservation of New England Antiquities. Visiting the museum I found Mr. Appleton, but instead of giving me information he asked me to help him classify the boxes on his shelves. At that time I met the

Plate 3. Up under the eaves — Beginning of the Museum.

[3]

Plate 4. A corner in the hallway — showing box collection.

curator, the late George Francis Dow, and discussed with
him the material for an article on the pantry for *Old Time
New England,* the monthly magazine of that society. The
article appeared before the one in the *New York Sun.*

Inspired by each new contact, I began to collect any utensil or implement which had seen service in the old kitchens,
sheds and barns. My collection rapidly increased and by
1935 I was becoming known as a connoisseur of the history
of early American crafts. My profession of music began to
slip away and this hobby became my second vocation, bringing to me lectures, exhibits and museum work.

It was not long after my first articles were published that
my correspondence began with William B. Sprague, an out-
standing collector of New York, now deceased. Mr. Sprague
sent me an old receipted bill, dated 1841, with several
wooden articles pictured in the upper corner, labeled as
wooden ware. This gave me the proper name of WOODEN
WARE for my collection. At about the same time Howard
G. Hubbard, then curator of Skinner's Museum in South

[4]

Hadley, met me and we passed many hours in discussing primitives and early history, and many letters went between us. A third correspondent was Mr. Frank K. Swain of Doylestown Museum, Doylestown, Pennsylvania. His letters were most instructive and his knowledge generously given. These three men not only stimulated and inspired me but gave me faith in myself. They had many years of experience back of them and I was a beginner.

It would be hard to say how and where the material for this book was gathered. From my childhood I have been interested in early manners, customs, and sayings, and have retained as I have learned. It was natural, then, that wherever I went as a collector I questioned and listened, and no chance remarks slipped by unheeded. A notebook went with me and I began to keep a diary of the happenings of the days.

Among my esteemed friends was a great-grandmother of eighty-seven. When I began collecting I would take any unusual piece to her and ask her to tell me how it was used

Plate 5. Three fine tankards, staved and hooped. The handle was made in one piece with a stave.

in the old days. She gave me vivid pictures of her girlhood and young womanhood days on a farm "down East" and often wrote down for me stories telling little incidents that only those of the older generations experienced.

While collecting, I chanced upon four men from different walks of life and living in remote sections, each eager to be of assistance in helping me understand about wooden ware. One of these is a typical settler, with a sharp memory and versed in innumerable trades. A second has a trained mind and, well versed in antiques, saved me from many an error and supplied me with much information. The third friend is a cooper from England and, while chalking patterns on his shop floor, taking me through a modern cooper shop and explaining to me the tools and many processes, he found me to be an eager pupil. The fourth friend is a wood-turner who supplied me with samples of the common woods.

As the book began to shape itself in 1936, these friends gave me material that could not be found on the printed page. Without their generous aid, this book would be far from complete.

There are four books to which I turned for reference — *Home Life in Colonial Days* by Alice Morse Earle (the name Earle has no immediate connection with my family name), *Every Day Life in Massachusetts Bay Colony* by George Francis Dow, *Ancient Carpenter's Tools* by Henry C. Mercer, and *The Community Industries of the Shakers* by Edward D. Andrews. This last book appeared after I had begun my work. I searched the bulletins of the United States Department of Agriculture and the monthly magazine called the *New England Farmer,* published from 1822 to 1846, and there I found additional information.

It should be more than a passing remark when I say that, with a few exceptions, I have taken all of the pictures myself, not from choice but to be able to say that the work was all my own. In the beginning I was coached by my brother, who had an old folding kodak, of the vintage of 1905, which he had rigged up with a bulb and with a screw hole for a tripod. This, plus a portrait attachment and a flood light, was my total equipment. No one knows the strain of accuracy in photography unless he has gone through it himself.

As we look back in the early history of America, we find there were three groups of colonists which settled in three widely separated localities. The first was the Virginian Colonists who settled in Jamestown in 1607; the New England Colonists settled in Plymouth in 1620, and the Pennsylvania Dutch, under William Penn, founded Philadelphia in 1683. The ways of all three colonies — their living, their manners and their costumes — were different for two distinct reasons: inheriting different traits from their ancestors from across the water, and living in different physical environments. The mild climate of Virginia brought one style of houses and living; the rigid climate of New England brought forth houses for comfort and furnishings of enforced severity, while the densely wooded sections of Pennsylvania produced log homes and stone houses with decorated furnishings such as came from the old country.

So we find a slight difference in wooden ware used in the different sections. That from the south and north varied but little — crude, simple and sturdy. The Dutch and the Germans of Pennsylvania were given more to decoration. The tulip pattern seemed to prevail, much as the pineapple prevailed in New England. But decoration was simple and, as Mr. Swain says, the people "decorated construction" and did not "construct decoration." Their ways of cooking varied from the New Englanders and thus utensils and implements varied accordingly. But fundamentally, wooden ware (or *treen* ware, as it was called, from *treen,* the plural of tree) was constructed with primitive tools, and for simple ways of living, from the trees found at hand.

I wish to express my appreciation to the publishers of the *New York Sun,* the *Magazine Antiques, Old Time New England, Hobbies, The American Collector,* and *Yankee* for their courtesies in publishing my articles from time to time.

With many happy memories of places I have visited, of acquaintances I have made, of hospitality shown me by those of an older generation and of interesting correspondence with all parts of the United States, I have written my book.

This enlarged edition has been made possible by more research work and by helpful correspondence from those interested in recording this early history. A few more pieces of wooden ware have come to the museum which now numbers over 1,000 pieces, including the iron fireplace utensils.

The entire collection of wooden ware, iron and tin ware now numbers twelve hundred pieces. The pictures which I took are catalogued and number one thousand negatives.

MARY EARLE GOULD

Worcester, Massachusetts, June, 1962

CHAPTER ONE

Earmarks on Wooden Ware

THE charm of a collection of wooden ware comes from the fact that in those early days every man created his own utensils and implements. But to understand such pieces one must visualize the ways of living and the daily labors of those early Colonists. Knowing that they baked in brick ovens, dried apples on racks, shelled corn on the edge of a shovel, made soap from the lye of the fireplace ashes, made their own butter, cheese, maple sugar and cider, ground their salt, spices, herbs and grains — knowing all this suggests the utensils and implements necessary for those daily labors.

COMPARING THE NEW AND THE OLD

Today, wooden ware is still being made and sold. It has a legitimate place, but it does not interest a collector. There is something about it that indicates it has come from a factory and is machine-made. In comparing the new and the old ware, such as plates, bowls and buckets, several things are noticeable in contrast. There is a feel in old wood just as there is in old glass or china. Age brings a softness and a lightness, and wear brings a smoothness. And more than that, there is a sound to old wood as there is a ring to old glass. The new wooden plate or bowl is fresh and not mellowed by time and no amount of varnish or shellac can disguise the fact.

The marks of the tool or a lathe are different in the new and the old wooden ware. The plate or bowl of today bears sharp marks of the lathe, and the staves of a bucket are very unfinished as they leave the machine. The old utensils were all done by hand with the drawknife, or a jackknife, or with hand tools while being held on a lathe, and the hand labor is easily detected in contrast to machine cutting.

Still another evidence of the difference between the new and the old ware is found in the nails and screws. Wooden pegs made by hand, nails forged on the anvil, and screws threaded by hand machinery, all belong to a period ante-dating factories. The hoops on the new buckets are lapped and fastened with machine-made nails, and the handle is set on in a less careful manner. The old hoops were first tucked under or set into each other, making a join which was called a locked lap. Later they were lapped and fastened with hand-forged nails or brads. The peg in the handle was fastened with another peg or was spliced, both ways affording a better hold than that of today's factory-made product.

Much of the old wooden ware shows crude workmanship. No two sides are alike, the cutting is uneven, pencil marks show how the work was planned, either with the compass or with a ruler, and there is no evidence of final polishing. Today, factories put out their wares in lots, while the handy man of long ago whittled his pieces one by one, sitting by the fire or in the barn door.

SOME OF THE EARMARKS

The word "earmarks" is used because of the custom of branding cows by a mark on the ear. Hence, earmarks is a fitting word in describing the characteristic marks on wooden ware.

One has to examine wooden ware carefully to detect ear-marks and must use his imagination to tell the purpose for which the articles were made. Much in the collection was named only after careful deductions. There is a large mor-tar, standing twenty-one inches high, with a yard-long pestle made from a hickory sapling. The end of the pestle is stained to a depth of eight inches. It is a stain of oil, and the odor proves it to be barley. The stain of barley never leaves wood, and this explains the purpose for which the mortar was used.

It is delightful to open a spice box and smell the still-lingering fragrance. Spices have been left in many of the boxes, but even when the box is empty a spicy odor remains. The oil of cloves, besides leaving an odor, also penetrates the wood and darkens it.

Salt and sugar leave dampness which penetrates the wood, a dampness which returns to the surface with every moist spell. A sugar box was purchased and taken from a dry shed. It was placed on the grass for the duration of an auction, when it was discovered that the dampness of the ground had penetrated the bottom of the box and brought out the old sugar stain, not only on the bottom of the box but on the cover as well. This dampness returns with the moisture of every summer.

Salt has a glisten, and tiny particles of it are found in the old salt boxes or bowls. A collector of wooden ware who would dry out boxes or buckets may profit by following a custom of Cape Cod folk who dry out wet rubber boots by allowing oatmeal to stand in them overnight.

There is a stain on all utensils and implements used in making butter. The bowl that held grease until there was enough for a batch of soap is very dark. Apple juice leaves a dark stain, and this shows on the wooden apple parers and on the splint baskets which were used for drying sliced apples. A cider press rack is stained over the entire frame and is very dark from the running juice.

A slatted rack was purchased and represented as being an apple drying rack. A connoisseur took up the point with me that the entire rack was dark from the stain of juice. A drying rack would be stained only on one side and not with running juice. This discussion led me to writing the former owner whose address I had been given. The reply came back that the rack was one belonging to a cider press but that it had also been used for holding sliced apples while resting on hooks over the stove. All of us were right — the dealer, the connoisseur, and myself.

On the other hand, soap bleaches. The soap stick, the clothes stick, the pounding stick, the wash board, the primitive scrubbing stick, and the dish drainer, are bleached from the lye in soap. Milk and cheese also bleach, and the bowls in which milk stood or in which cheese was strained are whitened.

The dye sticks and the dye tub are stained and colored. The hasty-pudding stick has a line that tells how deep the pudding was in the kettle. Flour dust clung to the wood and whitened it. The scoop which took the flour from the barrel, the long paddle which stirred the dough in the big troughs, and the long knife which cut the dough into loaves, show their purpose.

When collecting wooden utensils one must also notice a third type of earmark — the wear. Much history may be learned by discovering how, and for what purpose, a piece was used. Many wooden plates are cut and scratched on the under side, which upholds the story that the top side was the dinner side and the under side the pie side!

There is an Indian eating scoop which was made to fit the hand — that of a large man, to judge by its size. There are teeth marks along one edge which show how the scoop was gripped in the hand and used to convey food to the mouth.

Some scoops are worn on the side, while others are snubbed at the end. The dipper, the sour cream scoop and the skimmer are worn on the end. Scoops are found that were used by a left-handed person, with the worn side opposite to that used by a right-handed person.

Chopping knives were rapped on the edge of the tray after the chopping was done and grooves were made. One chopping tray shows that it was used by a left-handed per-

Plate 6. Left, dipper showing worn edge opposite handle. Center, this Indian eating scoop shows teeth marks on right-hand edge. Right, wall box for holding pumice used in cleaning knives. Marks on back show where knives were scoured.

son because of the position of the worn groove. Chopping trays or bowls — they were called by either name — were worn deep when in long service, and mortars vied with them in the every-day labors. A left-handed person made a scoop for himself with the nose on the side convenient for him. There is a nest of boxes with left-handed laps.

The pantry boxes fell into many uses. Some covers were turned over and used as cutting boards. There is one home today where cooking chocolate is still cut on the inside of the old box cover! Covers were often considered a good place for memoranda, and figures and sums were jotted down on

[13]

them. Even messages and addresses were sometimes written on them, much as with a friendship book. A cobbler
pulled out three nails from one of his boxes, put in his spools
of thread and ran the ends through the holes. This served
as his sewing box. Many boxes were used for jewelry, some
lined with calico and others with a scrap of cotton on the
bottom. The boxes were catch-alls — for everything from
scissors in the schoolroom to nails and screws in the sheds.

Wall boxes, in which knife polish was kept, have deep
grooves on the upright part that hung on the wall. The box
was laid flat on the table and the back was used as a support for the knives when they were scoured with pumice

Plate 7. Two water buckets and a wooden funnel. Bucket at left shows marks where
rapped with a dipper. One at right has worn edges from being overturned to dry.

stone. Some wall boxes are worn thin from the oft-repeated
operation. One such box was kept near the chimney, for
the back is scorched from the heat of the bricks.

Wash boards and the scrubbing stick are worn from rub-
bing, while the smoothing boards are darkened by friction
and show no sign of water. One smoothing board has two

[14]

Plate 8. Two winnowing sieves. One has a splintered edge.

grooves cut at the end where the fingers could have a better grip. This showed that it was a smoothing board and not a scrubbing stick as it was first thought to be.

A mute message to the collector is found in the sieves. Caught in the strands of the splint in the hoops of the winnowing sieves, husks of grain can be found, sometimes from oats and sometimes from wheat. Invariably each hoop is splintered all around the edge except in one spot. At this particular place there is a cord threaded through a hole by which the sieve hung. It was at this point that the hand gripped the rim when the sieve was rapped on the barn floor after the grain had been sifted. This freed the sieve of the remaining husks but it would not be many harvests before the rim of the sieve was splintered and broken. Even the cord broke in time. In the horsehair sieves of the Shakers, husks of herb seeds are still found in the mesh, but after too much curious handling these husks have disappeared. Even medicine powders have clung to the tiny sieves used in the preparation of medicine.

[15]

A tankard was found with a cork plugged into a hole in the cover. The dealer who had purchased it thought this hole was an imperfection and had carefully filled it with a cork and varnished over it. After digging out the cork it was discovered that the rim of the hole was charred and that once upon a time a hot toddy stick had been thrust through the hole to heat the toddy. It takes an inquisitive mind to ferret out meanings which may not be apparent to the casual observer.

The creative man of long ago makes us of today smile at some of his contrivances. An oblong chopping tray had

Plate 9. Upper left, tankard. Upper right, once a chopping tray, now a strainer and grater. Lower left, a pie peel made from part of a hand bellows. Lower right, two graters ingeniously constructed from one tin lantern.

worn through with hard usage. New England thrift would not allow it to be discarded, so the hole was cut larger and evenly and a piece of pierced tin was nailed over it. This addition made the tray serve two purposes — as a sieve and on the underside as a grater. In time this new utensil saw hard usage, and strips of iron, secured with hand-forged nails, kept the old chopping tray in service. An old lantern of pierced tin also went through a transformation. The door was made into a grater by nailing it on to a handle, while the lantern itself was used as another grater after a narrow board, serving as a handle, had been fastened into the space where the door belonged. Two graters in place of one lantern.

Some pieces are not easy to decipher. A pie peel was bought in perfectly good faith, yet suspicion as to its authenticity followed later. Careful examination showed a handle too good in workmanship; the end of the peel re-shaped; nail holes around the edge by the handle, and a greasy smear on the back. All of this led to the discovery that the peel had once seen service as a pair of bellows. A clever man had taken one part to make a pie peel. Perhaps the second part was put to use in still another way.

It is common to find that pestles wandered from their mortars and were used as mashers and even as hammers. Mashers, too, show nail prints.

Plate 9b. Three early wooden porringers.

[17]

CHAPTER TWO

Wood — What the Early Settlers Found and How They Learned to Use It to the Best Advantage

WHEN looking at wooden ware one of the first points that comes to mind has to do with wood. What is the wood from which the articles were made? How did the early settlers know what to use? And how did they know when to cut the trees?

The Indian taught the white man much of his wood lore and the white man soon learned for what purposes the trees could be used. There was wood for dry purposes and for wet purposes, wood that bent easily for hoops, box rims and wheel rims, wood that was soft and cut easily, and wood that was hard and durable, wood that had resilience and wood that was ornamental. All of this knowledge came from the Indians and from the white man's own experience.

THE EARLY FORESTS

Dense forests spread over the land when the early settlers came to these shores. In a letter written by Benjamin Rush to Thomas Jefferson in 1791, it was stated that six thousand maple trees were destroyed in clearing the average farm in New York or Pennsylvania. That could quite logically be called the wood age, for there followed a long period during which nearly everything was made of wood, from door hinges and water pipes to household furnishings and utensils.

In the old farm magazines many superstitions are recorded in regard to cutting timber. All sciences have been founded on observation. Nature has been closely observed by man and sayings of great wisdom have been passed down by word of mouth and later recorded as scientific facts.

It seems that the moon has great influence on both Nature and man, and the scientist can readily believe the many strange deductions made long ago. From 1778 comes the saying that timber should be cut by the traditional "old moon in February." At the same time we read that timber, cut in the wane of the moon, was much more durable than if cut between the new moon and the full moon. "The moon has such potential influence in the various parts of her orbits, that by cutting one tree three hours before the new moon and another of the same kind of tree six hours afterwards, a difference in the soundness of the timber would be noticed."* This seems to signify that the moon had an influence on the sap of the tree and the flowing of the sap, and hence the cutting of the tree was judged with great accuracy.

There were several quite recognizable reasons for cutting timber in February by the "old moon." With no leaves on the trees the cutting of timber was easier; with snow on the ground the task of removing the timber was simplified. Another important advantage was that wood would dry quickly in the March winds.†

Cutting timber for poles and splint was done in May when the sap was running vigorously. At this time the bark begins to spread and becomes looser and can be easily removed, a difficult task at other times. Poles for wellsweeps, hoops, wheel rims, and similar purposes, were also cut and peeled in May when the live wood contained the maximum amount of oil, which contributed to the wood its necessary

*The New England Farmer.

†The cause of March winds is explained by the fact that as the sun's rays become more intense, following the winter season, the frozen ground thaws and the moisture evaporates. This moisture rises and strikes the layer of cool air and causes a vacuum, into which rushes the surrounding air. This causes the winds of March, and at no other time of the year does this take place for a prolonged period.

quality of give-and-take. Sap does not run as vigorously after the shade comes and covers the roots. By July the heat is intense, and by October the sap begins to run back again. This explains the choosing of definite times for cutting timber — March, April and May.

STRUCTURE OF TREE

The structure of the tree is much like that of the human being. There are two principal roots, the tap root and the sap root. The tap root, from which the trees' growth emanates, supplies the heart or core of the tree, corresponding to the marrow in the human bone. The sap root supplies the sap, which runs up the outer surface of the tree and out along the branches, as does the blood stream in the human body. These two sections distinctly show in full-grown trees. Young trees, or saplings, have no heart.

GROWTH OF TREE

The growth of the tree depends on location, soil and exposure. Trees that are too crowded draw less nourishment from the soil and get less sunshine. The branches, whose function it is to take in the oxygen and promote growth, have little opportunity to reach the light and sun. Planted apart, as Benjamin Franklin instructed in one of his numerous bits of advice, the trees grow more rapidly and stronger. Pine trees, say tree students, grow tall and take oxygen at the top, drawing the air upwards, which tends to make the forest cold. Maple trees spread out and take the oxygen at all points, thus making the forest warmer.

The north side of the tree is retarded by lack of sun, while the south side shows more growth. This is shown in the formation of the rings, the rings being closer together on the north side and wider and farther apart on the south side.

Each year a new ring forms, and the more slowly the tree grows the less will be the breadth of the ring and closer will be the grain of the wood, and the harder the wood will be. These rings also indicate the seasons. Drought is shown by close, narrow rings, while moisture in normal or rainy seasons produces a quicker growth. Trees growing slowly are easier to fell and cut while those with large annual rings are twice as tough and strong. The slow-growing trees make durable timber, while the wood of fast-growing trees has greater flexibility.

METHODS OF CUTTING TIMBER

The first sawing was done in sawpits and the practice is still carried on in some uncivilized countries. A pit was dug in the ground and covered with spaced logs, making a platform on which the logs were sawed. A long, two-handled saw was used, one man standing in the pit and one man standing on the platform.

There were, and still are, two ways commonly employed in the cutting of timber. The one most commonly used was the plain-sawed, or flat-grained, method which consisted of sawing the log in parallel layers beginning with the outside. The other was that of quarter-sawing. By this method the log was first cut lengthwise into quarters and then boards or planks cut alternately from the face of each quarter, or in some instances diagonally, 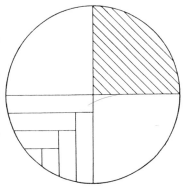 depending upon the grain effect desired. (See illustration.) Besides showing the grain more advantageously, the quarter-sawed lumber would warp relatively less.

The most important woods found in the early forests were maple, pine, birch, ash, oak, beech, hickory, black walnut, cedar, poplar, and basswood. Apple, cherry, elm and willow were also found in various sections, but because they were little used for wooden ware they are not described here.

Maple — Sugar, or rock, maple was the most common of the trees and served many purposes. Sugar was not the least of these, becoming as it did a most important article in the homes. Maple was the most valuable firewood in the whole forest, and backlogs of this wood — from fifteen to twenty inches in diameter and five feet long — were in constant demand. As ninety per cent of heat went up the chimney, a large supply of wood was always on hand. The ashes from the maple were valued as fertilizer and in the making of soap.

Maple is the most common wood found in household ware. Rolling pins, mashers, stirrers, bread boards, butter prints and molds, chopping bowls, ladles, spoons, and all common ware, were maple. One John Lawson wrote from Carolina in 1714 that in that region dishes, trenchers, and spinning wheels were made from maple, and the Iroquois Indians of New York also made paddles, spoons and ladles from this hard wood.

Maple has a satiny appearance with a distinct fleck in the grain. It is a slow-growing tree, so the rings are close together, and when cut across the grain, the marks are like dashes and dots of a deeper color. The curly maple is more decorative, and its flecks are in curves or broken circles, and in the crosscut there is a pronounced wavy grain.

Bird's-eye maple is an accidental formation. The young wood is disturbed each season by the presence of buds which are unable to force their way to the surface. Thus the wood is forced to grow around these obstructions, making irregular rings. As the saw cuts through these abnormal growths the crumpled edges closely resemble the eyes which characterize this wood. For this reason it is most decorative for tables, chairs, bureaus and beds. An occasional bowl and box is found made of bird's-eye maple.

Because of its hardness, smoothness and attractive color, maple was used in wooden ware and cooperage — for pantry boxes, sieves, rims, cheese and butter boxes, tubs and pails, bowls, mortars, as well as for pantry tools. The shoe cobbler made his last and supports from maple, and the wooden pegs, which were used in fastening boxes, were of this maple when birch could not be obtained.

Pine — Early settlers found the coast densely wooded with pine. They began cutting timber at once and by 1635 were sending masts to England. In thirty years, in 1650, they were trading timber to Madagascar and to Guinea for slaves, to the Canary Islands for wine, and to Cuba and Haiti for sugar. By 1721 Massachusetts was launching from one hundred and forty to one hundred and sixty vessels annually. Bridges as well as homes were built of pine. More could be done with pine, and with less effort, than with any of the other woods. Floors, ceilings, paneling, inside blinds, shelves, and much furniture, such as benches, stools, chairs, tables, bedsteads and cupboards, were made of this wood.

White Pine was used for covers and bottoms of cheese boxes and butter boxes. There was no odor and no taste to this pine, a necessary thing to consider in choosing wood which was to come in contact with food. Staves of buckets and tubs and small kitchen utensils, all made by the white cooper, were of this pine. Even when constantly wet, the pine wood did not decay. Pine is light in weight and light in color. It is a slow-growing tree, and the rings are close together with no flecks or breaks.

Pitch Pine, or hard pine, was found to be another useful tree. From this wood splinters or spills were made to serve as tapers for light. Pitch pine knots were used for out-of-door lighting at nighttime. A framework cage of iron on the end of a pole held them as they burned, and they lighted the way when the settlers were hunting deer or fishing. Gathering pine knots was as carefully attended to as was the cutting of the winter's wood or the cribbing of corn. This was done in the fall of the year when the pines had fallen and decayed and the knots could be easily cut. In New York state, tar taken from the fallen pitch pine knots became one of the important industries.

Birch — The birch was another abundant tree, and Maine rated it second in stand among the hardwoods. The white birch, called paper birch, canoe birch or silver birch, is light, hard and tough. It grows where scarcely any other tree will survive. Birch wood is lighter in color than maple and the grain is closer. The wood has a satiny look, with light and dark waves running diagonally; the flecks short and small.

The inner silk bark of the white birch was used as paper for windows and later for letter writing, before real paper was made. Canoes were made of this birch, giving it the name of canoe birch. The wood was taken green because there was much oil in it and it therefore shed water. Broom makers used the twigs, tying them to a birch handle, and the Indian's splintered broom, later made by the settlers, was made from the birch saplings. Hoop benders used the larger branches. Clothespins, pail handles, staves and hoops, boxes and washboards are found made from birch. The birch pegs for the pantry boxes, used originally for shoe pegs, were made by hand until about 1818 when Joseph Walker of Massachusetts invented a machine for their manufacture.

Birch branches were used to heat the bake ovens because

they burned slowly and gave out great heat. The sticks could be removed with an iron ash peel before they became ashes. Because of this same slow-burning quality, birch was used in making charcoal. In this case the sticks were charred after smoldering in covered mounds for several days. And birch ashes were used in obtaining lye for use in soap and bleaching clothes.

Ash ranks next in value to that of oak for strength and durability and it is adapted to a much wider range of uses than oak. The wood is white, tough, hard and resilient, qualities which were much valued by wheelwrights, cartwrights, cabinet makers and wood turners. The second growth was used as much as the first growth. Ash is a fast-growing tree and the rings are wide and regular, though in broken lines. Trees which grow rapidly are the most valued as timber because they have a characteristic toughness to a high degree. Black ash, called swamp ash because of the places in which it grew, was used for hoop poles. The young shoots were cut, when about one and one-half inches in diameter, into long lengths and tied together in bunches with hickory or birch withes. They were sold or traded to a cooper to be used for barrel and keg hoops. Many a poor farmer could make extra money by his "hoop poles." The full-grown tree of black ash was used for splint.

Hickory — The name has its derivation from an Indian name — *Pawhiccora*. This name was given to the milk or oily liquid which was pressed from the pounded nuts of the tree. In 1653 *pohickory* is listed among the trees in Virginia. This was finally shortened to *hickory*. Occasionally the name walnut is given to several species of hickory in New England. The shagbark is a variety of hickory, and is so-called from its shaggy covering. The best of our hickory nuts come from the shagbark.

Hickory is similar to ash in appearance, both in weight and in color, and has faintly marked rings which are much broken. The small shoots were used for hoops and for splint as was swamp ash. Often the bark was left on the small hickory saplings when used as barrel hoops.

When the trees were cut in the spring of the year, several ash and hickory trees were singled out and hauled into the yard to be used for splint. As the sap was running at that time, the wood was more porous. Trees for splint were singled out and marked as were the trees for masts, from four to twelve feet in diameter. The tree was quartered and the wood pounded with a wooden mallet called a beetle. A heavy drawknife was used to pull off strips which went the full length of the tree. The ash made strips eight or ten inches wide, while the hickory made narrower strips. These were put into a nearby brook or pond, weighted down and left until needed, when they were cut to the necessary width and shaved to a usable thinness.

The Indians taught the settlers this wood lore. They made baskets of all kinds and descriptions, from the large, tall ones for potatoes to the small ones for general utility. They would come to a settlement with their baskets to trade them for food or any commodity which they lacked. Trading then seemed to be the only means of supplying one's need, and history records many interesting deals — from the trading of Long Island to that of butter and eggs. In due time the settler was making his own articles — clam baskets, cheese baskets, apple-drying baskets, utility baskets, winnowing baskets, winnowing sieves, charcoal sieves, as well as splint seats for chairs. The splint pieces illustrated show remarkable workmanship and durability. The use of splint is more fully explained in another chapter.

The Oak, like the ash, had no odor and bent easily. Rims

of box covers, sides of larger boxes for butter, sugar and meal, and bucket hoops and bail handles are found in oak. Cheese presses and butter churns were made of oak. The first trestle table that served as an eating table was made of oak, the huge trees supplying very wide planks. These were spoken of as "oaken boards," or "table bords" a common expression in the old lore. A trencher in the collection, measuring fourteen inches and dated 1770, is supposedly English oak and very rare. The base of an oak tree was often used for large grain mortars, and oak was used for staves in the barrels that held liquids and in well buckets.

Oak was the heaviest native wood and was less apt to be eaten by the powder-post beetle than the other woods. It is darker than ash and heavier and has a less pronounced grain, which is broken. The rings are far apart as the tree is fast-growing. When the wood is quartered, the grain shows patches, marked like watered ribbon. This is very decorative, as is the curly or bird's-eye maple, and many butter boxes are made of this quartered wood.

Beech, next to the maple, is one of the prettiest of woods. It is a hard wood, and heavy, and has a deeper color than maple. The rings show as broken flecks and when cut cross-wise there are satiny dashes running at right angles to the grain. These markings and the reddish color are the distinguishing characteristics of beech. Rolling pins, scoops and boxes were made from this most decorative wood. Beech is not affected by water and has no taste, which would be the main reasons for its use in wooden ware. When constantly wet, it would be sound after as many as forty years. Beech tree leaves made better mattresses than straw or chaff and the blue beech was used in making splintered brooms.

Chestnut was used in the same manner as these other woods for bowls, boxes and ware that had hard usage. It was not so commonly used, however, as it was more easily eaten by the powder-post beetle. Chestnut is about the color of oak, but it is very light in weight, averaging the same per cubic foot as the pine, poplar and willow. Being a fast-growing tree, the rings are far apart. The grain has an irregular, rough formation that shows in sketchy waves.

Black Walnut was not used to any great extent for wooden ware, but in Pennsylvania, where the tree was more common than on the coast, an occasional utensil has been found made of this wood. The black walnut is related to the butternut. The nuts of both species were used commercially, the husks in dyeing and tanning and the nuts for eating.

Walnut was easy to work and took a beautiful polish. The color is brown, not a red brown like mahogany, and the grain is made up of close, fine checks. The burl was used and made very ornamental articles. Black walnut, however, is more generally associated with furniture than with utensils.

Cedar — There were three species of cedar growing in different localities which were used in wooden ware. The southern white cedar, the northern white cedar and the red.

The southern white cedar was used by a class in Philadelphia known as cedar coopers. From it were made churns, pails, firkins, keelers, piggins and washtubs. It was a smooth wood, light in weight, had great strength, and resisted decay.

The northern white cedar was used in the same manner in the localities in which it grew. It was used also by early settlers of eastern Pennsylvania and New Jersey in making a rheumatism ointment by bruising the leaves and molding them with lard.

The red cedar is known especially for its use in chests and in coffins. The Indians never used this wood for fire purposes because it burned slowly and with little blaze. Red cedar has a lasting quality and was used in cooperage.

Poplar has been called whitewood because of its whiteness. It is soft, has an even texture and is easily worked. Having no taste or odor it was popular in bowls, plates, spoons and scoops. The wood looks like pine except that it is whiter and lighter.

Basswood is called poplar in Ohio, whitewood in Massachusetts and linden in Pennsylvania, besides being called spoonwood in certain other localities. It is very white in color and when left unfinished has a colorless appearance. It is light and soft, easily worked, but lacks strength and wearing quality.

Mahogany was brought to this country at an early date from the West Indies and Central America. Sir Walter Raleigh went ashore at Trinidad in 1597 and used native mahogany for repairing his vessel. One hundred years later a Captain Gibbons took some mahogany to England as ballast. The captain's brother was erecting a house and attempted to use the timber in construction, but found it too hard to work. Wollaston, a cabinetworker with Captain Gibbons, used a piece in making a box — not the kitchen variety of box — and the beauty was immediately appreciated. He then made a bureau and his reputation as a cabinetmaker became established. Mahogany was, and is, used primarily for furniture. There are many species, and because of the color the wood is sometimes confused with lignum-vitæ.

Lignum-vitæ is the heaviest wood known. Like mahogany it was imported from the West Indies and Central America. The sap wood and the heart wood of lignum-vitæ show a sharp contrast, the sap wood being very light in color and the heart very dark. When the wood is taken at the line of these two the combination is very beautiful and ornamental. Mortars, rolling pins and chopping bowls were made from the combined sections. In England, sand shakers, called sand-ers, were made of this striped part, and those that are in collections here were brought over many years ago. This contrast in wood was found only in old trees. The young ones had no heart, being all sap wood, and this accounts for the light-colored lignum-vitæ. Similar utensils made from the sap wood seem so totally different from those made from the heart wood that were it not for the extreme weight one might question the wood. If lignum-vitæ is stained it can look like mahogany. Illustrations of two handleless rolling pins, a chopping bowl and two mortars, one mortar show-ing both the sap wood and the heart in contrasting streaks, are shown in Plate 75.

Sour Gum Tree — One other tree quite necessary in wooden ware was the tupelo, of the dogwood family. The name was a native American Indian name and the tree was called "black gum," "sour gum" and "pepperidge." The wood has a curly grain and is very difficult to split. As the tree ages, it becomes hollow and for that reason was used with great advantage in making the first barrels and large pounding mortars.

THE CUTTING OF TREES

The trees were felled, stripped of branches and limbs and cut into lengths as logs. These were hauled on scoots by oxen to the banks of a nearby river, and stacked in piles away from the water's edge. Scoots were vehicles with two low runners, across which was laid a floor of thick planks. Piles were held in iron rings at the sides and these in turn held the logs. The logs were run up onto the scoots on skids which were two logs acting as rails. When spring came, the logs were pushed into the river and floated down-stream to the saw mill, where they were sawed according to the owner's direction, some for furniture, some for planks and boards and some for the smaller articles. At the time the trees were cut, several were hauled into the dooryard and left to weather. These were to be used, at the owner's convenience, for wooden ware and splint.

Wood in the early days was barked and air-dried and all the properties preserved, whereas today the too rapid artificial drying in kilns makes wood much inferior in quality. This contrast is well shown in the old unpainted weather-beaten houses, still standing, which were built two hundred or more years ago. The wood used in these houses contained its natural properties and no paint was needed to preserve it from the elements. The passerby wonders at its remarkable state of preservation until the explanation is given.

The wood that went to the sawmill had either been sold outright or was to be kept by the owner, who paid for his own cutting. This bill was called a "saw bill." The owner either took his boards, staves and pine pieces home to use himself or, if he was not skillful enough, carried them to the cooper. The cooper would make a certain number of barrels and buckets for a specific amount of wood given him in trade. "Down east" the transaction was described in the words, "They traded a bargain." We should remember that trading was one of the first instincts of man, and that the early Americans' trading or bartering was done with butter, cheese and produce from the farm.

THE COOPER

The cooper was the handy man of the village, more or less skillful with his hands. He set up his shop in his own home, in a shed or in the lean-to, or built a small shop out in the yard. His work was called *coopering* or *cooperage*. There was the *wet* or *tight* cooper who made barrels and casks for liquids, using white oak. This work required the most skill. The *dry* or *slack* cooper made barrels for flour and sugar, for which he used red oak, maple, elm, ash, hickory, and chestnut. The white cooper made small pieces, such as buckets, tubs and staved boxes, and butter churns, using pine, beech, maple, birch and hickory. This white cooper made the pantry tools and the nests of boxes and even the wooden bowls and plates, for there were many homes where no man was clever enough with his hands or who had time or inclination to make things for the kitchen. The eating bowls and plates were called turner's ware, for they were made on a lathe. The men who made this particular ware were called *dish turners*. There was also the *traveling cooper* who made his seasonal rounds, carrying with him his tools, staves and hoops. He repaired whatever was necessary — washing and brewing utensils, and churns and buckets for the dairy.

Coopering dates back to 70 A. D. At the time when the *Mayflower* came over, coopers were a part of the crew, and later all ships that left for foreign ports had coopers and other tradesmen among the sailors. Gradually, each village had its cooper, and this custom continued until factories appeared where machinery turned out such products in large quantities for both home and distant trade. But in many localities and in isolated sections the men of the family continued to make their own house furnishings and the kitchen wooden ware, and this accounts for the crude workmanship found in many pieces.

COMPARATIVE WEIGHTS OF WOODS
PER CUBIC FOOT

	POUNDS		POUNDS
Apple	48	Larch	36
Ash	50	Lignum-vitæ	82
Basswood	38	Locust	46
Beech	50	Logwood	57
Birch	41	Mahogany	50
Boxwood	70	Maple (hard)	42
Cedar (red)	36	Oak (white)	52
Cherry (wild)	42	Oak (live)	56
Chestnut	35	Pine (white)	29
Cork	15	Pine (yellow)	38
Cypress	37	Poplar	31
Ebony	80	Rosewood	62
Elm	39	Spruce and Hemlock	42
Fir (Norway pine)	38	Sycamore	38
Gum (black)	42	Teak	52
Hickory	52	Walnut (black)	38
		Willow	33

Plate 9c. A bannock board on which cakes were baked in front of the fire.

CHAPTER THREE

Tools for Making Early Wooden Ware

WOODEN WARE came into existence when tools were in their primitive state. Very little was required to supply the homes of the Colonists, and what little wooden ware was needed called for simple tools.

It has been said that the oldest known invention of man was the wheel. One can rightly say that a tool of some kind was the oldest invention, for it was with a tool that a wheel was made. Tools have been traced so far back that it seems as if they must have appeared soon after the creation of man. Man has always been reaching for something new to enable him to live more easily and comfortably, and in order to prosper and progress he has been forced to make tools with which to work.

THE INDIANS' TOOLS

The Indian on the North American shores had little variety in the tools with which he made his homes and his furnishings. Nature had given him wood, flint, stone, bone and shell, and with these he fashioned the tools necessary for his existence. But the living customs of the white man were more elaborate than those of the Indians, and the tools he required became more numerous and complicated.

The Indians had a tool called an adze which they made from flint. This was nothing more than a short, chubby-shaped head that was sharp at one end, similar to an axe head. This hollowed out wood most laboriously, chipping pieces no larger than sawdust. The Indians used this adze in making their canoes, first charring the wood with fire, which made it cut more easily. There is a canoe in the National Museum in Washington that is 59 feet long, with

8-foot beam, 7-foot 3-inch bow, and 5-foot 3-inch stern. This carried one hundred persons and their outfits, and was longer by 19 feet than the *Sparrow Hawk* that brought settlers from England to America in 1626.

With this same adze the Indian made his beautiful burl bowls, which are now prized so highly. The burl was the wart or tumor on trees, the best burls growing on maple and ash trees. The characteristic bowl of the Indians, showing clearly the marks of the hand tools, was the deep oval one with handle holes.

THE COOPERS' TOOLS

The cooper of the seventeenth and eighteenth centuries had tools bearing the same names as the tools of today, but certain of their tools were made in different forms. There was an adze like that of the Indians, but instead of being just a head of flint it consisted of an iron head with a wooden handle. There were adzes of several sizes and shapes and they were used to hollow out bread troughs, bowls and ladles and the large mortars used for grain. Then there were the hammers, axes, hatchets, saws, knives, a spokeshave similar to a carpenter's plane, a stock and bit, and an auger and gimlet — all like those of today.

Two tools that were used in making barrels and tubs were the scorp, or scorper, and the croze. The scorp was a curved blade of steel on a forked end of a wooden handle. It was used to smooth the inside edges of the staves after the barrel, keg or bucket was finished. The handle was of different lengths, according to the depth of the receptacle being made. The croze was a semi-circular instrument with a handle at right angles. There were many sizes for the different barrels and kegs. It had an adjustable saw-like attachment which cut grooves in the end of the staves into which the heads fitted.

Two tools were used when making the heads of the barrels and the bottoms of the kegs and buckets. One was the divider, also called the gauge or compass. This marked the circle for the size of the head, which was then cut with a shave. The other tool was the chamfer which beveled the edge of the heads and bottoms while they were held in a vise.

The frow and the beetle, as well as the drawknife, were found in every workshop or shed. The frow was an iron blade set at right angles to a handle and the beetle was a heavy wooden mallet, sometimes banded with iron, with which the frow was struck and driven into the wood. These were used in splitting logs. This same wooden mallet was also used for driving the large pegs that held the beams of the houses and barns, and even used to open barrels. If used for knocking in barrel heads, it was called a bung starter. The drawknife was used for drawing or peeling off strips when making splint, and, like the modern jack-knife, was used for whittling.

THE LATHE

Besides the tools, a necessary part of the equipment for making wooden ware was the lathe. On this were made plates, bowls, mortars, sugar bowls, noggins, butter prints, pestles, parts of the cheese press, the butter churn plunger and any odd parts of pantry tools. There are two old engravings which show the lathe in operation, one printed in the thirteenth century giving the date of the first lathe as 1290, and the other printed in the seventeenth century. In the first engraving a man is seated at a lathe turning a bowl. The picture is from an old Latin manuscript. The second engraving was done by Jan Joris Van Vliet, a Dutchman born in 1610. In that engraving there is a shelf on the wall back of the lathe on which there is a shoulder yoke, a butter box, and a keg or churn. This shows that tools such as the lathe were conceived to fashion wooden ware hundreds of years ago. The lathe-turned bowl seems such a perfect creation, it is hard to believe that it could have been in existence in the thirteenth century.

SPRING POLE LATHE

The first lathe was called the spring pole lathe, having but a few simple parts. There was an arm for holding the work, fastened between two posts on a standard, a foot treadle and a curved pole which was fastened to the ceiling. This was suspended by the middle so that it swayed up and down. A cord was tied to one end, wound around the work arm and carried down to the foot treadle. As the treadle was pressed, the arm turned, pulling down the pole over head. The pole sprang back when the treadle was released and the work arm returned to its first position. There was only a half-circle motion, not a full rotation. The cutting was done with chisel-shaped tools called turning tools, which were held in the hand, and there were many sizes and shapes. When one half of a piece was cut, the work was turned around and the other half done. Both the inside and the outside of the bowl were cut in this manner, and when the turning was finished there remained the blocks of wood on the bottom and the inside to be cut off by hand. This spring pole lathe was often set up out in the yard and a slender sapling became the overhead pole, springing back when the peddle was released. Those early workshops were commonly set up in the yard, doing away with the trouble of building suitable housing.

MANDREL LATHE

A later lathe of the seventeenth and eighteenth centuries was called a mandrel lathe. This had a continuous action.

This lathe was not wholly satisfactory as the arms were not always steady and the work wobbled, making it somewhat oval in shape. But as wood shrinks with age the lathe was not entirely responsible for the shape. Bowls and mortars were cut in many ornamental ways. The edges were beveled and groups of lines down the side show much thought and excellent art.

Things made on the lathes are called hand-made in distinction to machine-made things of the factories that followed later. A hand tool performed the work while the lathe held it.

NAILS

There is yet another thing to examine in wooden ware besides the wood and ear marks, and that is the nails. They are very important, but deductions from them are not always infallible. Old nails do not necessarily indicate old pieces. Hand-forged nails might have been lying around long after machine-clipped nails were being made. Moreover, certain isolated sections would have been using the old nails while factories in distant cities were putting out their products. There are even now old nails which could be used to fake antique pieces. But in general, the age of the nails helps in telling the period of wooden ware.

In the book, *Ancient Carpenter's Tools and Implements* by Dr. Hency C. Mercer, six kinds of nails are listed. They are nails with convex, hammered or rounded heads; nails with T-shaped heads; nails with inverted L-shaped heads; those that were headless; and tacks and spikes. In the pantry boxes there were nails with a spear point that could be flattened into a letter J. In the larger boxes and on the hoops that are lapped the nails have convex, hammered, rounded heads.

[38]

The Shakers' boxes are fastened with copper nails, both in the laps and at the rims where the cover and bottom join the sides. This is one of the characteristics of the Shaker boxes. The Colonists used anything they had on hand, and their boxes show a great variety. Where the Shakers used copper nails on the rims the Colonists used wooden cobbler's pegs. Factories began to appear in early 1800 and then came the boxes that are fastened in the lap with copper or iron tacks. Wooden pegs continued to be used in fastening the rims.

Nails were first imported from England, having been made there since the fifteenth century. In America, following the Revolutionary War, there was a scarcity of imported nails and the need of them called for home-made inventions. Many farmers set up little forges in the kitchen and made their own nails, to use in their own wooden ware. Nail making was a family affair with the children helping.

A flat iron bar from which the nail was made was called a "nailrod," measuring $1\frac{3}{4}$ inches wide and $3/16$ of an inch thick. The forge or small anvil was called a "bolster," a piece of steel about 10 inches long, $1\frac{1}{4}$ inches wide and $\frac{1}{2}$ inch thick. In it was a hole the size of the nail to be made, sometimes a second hole for a second nail of a different size. The nailrod was heated and shaped into a point by hammering on an anvil. A mass was left for the head and when this was inserted into the bolster and a section, the length to be the nail, cut off, the mass was pounded into a head. This made a great variety of irregular heads. The T-shaped head, long and narrow, was the common type.

The farmers were given the nailrods and in exchange for doing the work, they kept enough nails for themselves. Blacksmiths did this work along with other forging, more often than did the farmers.

Jeremiah Wilkinson of Cumberland, Rhode Island, adopted a plan for cutting tacks from sheet iron, with shears, in 1775. There was a method for cutting nails and heading them in a vise thought out by Ezekiel Reed of Bridgewater, Massachusetts, in 1786, and he took out a patent for a machine for cutting cold tacks and nails. Jacob Perkins of Newburyport, Massachusetts, invented the first machine to make a complete nail, a patent being issued to him January 16, 1785. A heading machine could head 6,000 brads an hour and a slotting machine many more than that.

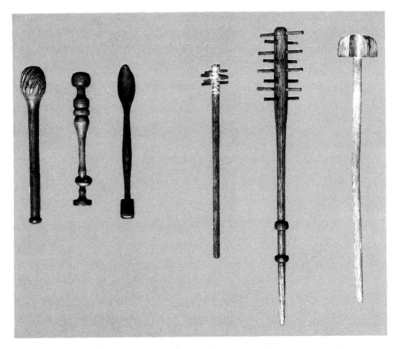

Plate 9d. On the left are three rare Swizzle Sticks to stir Swizzle -- a mixture of ale and beer. The sticks were grasped between the palms and spun or rotated. The three toddy sticks at the right crushed the lemon and sugar as well as stirred.

CHAPTER FOUR

Old New England Kitchens — How Our Ancestors Lived and Labored

A COLLECTION of wooden ware introduces to us the old New England kitchens. What did the kitchens look like? How did our ancestors cook in the fireplaces and bake-ovens? What were the dishes and the table? How we would like to turn back the pages of history and look into those kitchens!

The one-room structure of 1620 was built around a fireplace. It held only the bare necessities — it was many years before the Colonies could think of physical comfort. The homes of the eighteenth and nineteenth centuries saw the addition of rooms, a second floor and an attic, but throughout these changes the kitchen remained center of the homes.

The wide floor boards, laid when wood was plentiful, served to keep out the cold. An under floor was often built and the space between the two floors filled with broken shale, crushed shale, reeds and withes. This was called "wattle and daub" and was also used between the outside clapboarding and the inside sheathing of the walls of the house. Heavy oak beams were used when nothing counted but security and durability. From the one window, which gave but little light and prevented warm air from escaping, several windows developed, but even then glass was not plentiful and there was more sash than glass. Substitutes for glass were used in the first crude structures, and only the better homes afforded the glass, brought from England.

Pine paneling was used as sheathing, a further protection from the cold. Plaster did not become a general thing until another quarter century, although an occasional room was plastered for the extra warmth it afforded. This plaster was made from hair of cows' tails and horses' manes mixed with crushed clam shells. Dung was often used as a binder. As early as 1697, lime was discovered in the soil at New-bury, Massachusetts, kilns were built and the business of producing lime became a prosperous one. Paint made from clays in the soil was not used to any great extent until Revolutionary days, and the pine floors and paneling were left in their natural condition. Doors swung on wooden or leather hinges until hand-wrought iron ones were made, many years after the landing of the Pilgrims.

The chimneys of the early structures were built on the ground, resting on a foundation set into the dirt a foot or more in depth. Field stones and shale from the surround-ing land were used, although bricks were made within the first decade and used in seaport towns, where clay was commonly found in the soil.

Excavating for a cellar was not considered necessary and the first homes were built on the ground. Many of the early houses have a cellar merely for the two-room section and not for the additions that were put up in later years. Cellars were places of storage and were reached at first by entrances from the outside through the foundation.

The chimney base in the cellar is an interesting bit of research work and well repays those who can examine the early houses. Solid foundations or arches were built accord-ing to the fancy of the builder. A preserve closet, a smoke oven or an additional fireplace with ovens were also accord-ing to fancy and many were the ways of using the chimney base, built of shale, boulders or brick. This study has been carried on and a second book has been added to the series of early home life.

The chimney many times had a base 15 feet square, sup-ported by oaken lintels or slabs of shale to keep the structure true. The first-floor fireplace was the same size as the chimney base, including fireplace, bake oven and ash oven. This then tapered to a smaller size to adapt itself for a second-floor chamber fireplace, tapering again to the size of the outside chimney or shaft. The earliest houses have a large central chimney sitting astride the roof.

FIRST BRICKYARD

Salem had the first brickyard as early as 1629, and all along the coast clay was found for making the bricks. In nearby sections the fireplaces and chimneys were made of bricks while the houses inland from the coast continued to have field stones and shale. The brickwork began at the first floor level and the bricks were "laid in puddled clay" up to the roof. The exposed chimney above the ridgepole was made by setting the bricks with lime mixed with clay.

The first chimney was made of wood and called a "catted" chimney. Sticks were laid "cobhouse" fashion, meaning that they were laid two by two, forming a square, and this was daubed inside and out with clay. In 1631 a Thomas Dudley of Salem, in writing to the Countess of Lincoln in England, said: "Wee have ordered that noe man shall build his chimney with wood nor cover his house with thatch . . ." — showing the danger of fire.

FIREPLACES

Just as there are periods in furniture and fashions, so there came to be various changes in fireplaces. Those in the beginning were made with openings as wide as eight and ten feet, and this continued as long as wood was plentiful. Whole animals could be roasted in such a fireplace. In some instances a settle would be built at one side in the opening where children were accustomed to sit. The fireplace was not only wide but deep, and sometimes a small window with glass panes was built at the back, through which the passerby could see the welcoming flames and avail himself of the hospitality within, day or night. Fireplaces diminished in size as the years went on.

COOKING

All cooking was done in and over the fire. The first pole on which the pots and kettles hung was made of wood and called the "lug pole." Wood was considered a failure, however, when, after the pole had charred to a point of weakness, it let the meal down into the embers. So iron was then substituted and a Yankee invention brought about the "crane" called thus because it suspended from the side wall in such a manner that it could be swung out into the room. Various length hooks were used to hold the pots, from those of six inches to some of fifteen inches. A trammel was a hook which could be lengthened or shortened to accommodate the height of the fire and the size of the kettle. This was made of two pieces of iron, the end of one having a hook which set into the other which had notches. This arrangement was copied in wood and used for holding a candle, the whole suspended near the fireplace. In those first fireplaces, the pots and kettles stood on legs, raising them above the hot embers. If they swung on the crane, they had flat bottoms. Much later kettles had an extension which set into the stove hole.

There was quite an array of cooking and roasting utensils for the big fireplace, first brought from the old countries and later made by local blacksmiths. The position of a blacksmith in early history was very important as it was he who forged the fighting tools and for that reason the blacksmith was carefully guarded in times of war lest he be captured.

[44]

The kettles were of many sizes and shapes, and pots vied with the kettles in boasting of variety. Kettles have straight sides and no covers while pots have bulging sides and a cover. Brass and copper kettles were highly prized, coming as they did from across the water while the lowly iron kettle was often used in trade with the Indians. The first iron kettle made in the new country, rightly a pot, was fashioned on a mold made by Joseph Jenks of Lynn in 1646 and is said to be now in the hands of descendants.

Skillets were iron cooking utensils, standing on legs, with a protruding handle and there were many sizes and an occasional variety as to depth. The long handle of the fry pan measures three feet so that the housewife might stand away from the hot embers as she prepared dinner. Short-handled pans were called spiders and aside from those there were flat griddles which either hung on the crane by a hoop handle or stood on three legs. Gridirons were stands with grating on legs. They were both round and square and the early ones had a revolving head so that the food might be exposed to the fire on all sides. The long-legged stand was the trivet and this was used to hold food to keep it warm after it had been prepared. These trivets were often elab-orately made with brass tops with designs of flowers, or fig-ures and most generally a handle was added for lifting it.

A rare find was the iron rabbit roaster, coming from an old home with its background of history. Standing on its side in front of the fire, it held the two parts of a dressed rabbit. Jagged iron supports held the meat from slipping and a turned edge below caught the juices. The roaster measures 15 by 12 inches and has three-inch protruding extensions at each corner. The fact that it has two frame supports instead of four legs shows that it did not stand in a flat position but tipped on its side.

A busy utensil was the iron toaster for bread or cheese. These were hand wrought and are exquisite examples of the fine work done by skillful blacksmiths. The head pivots on the base which rests on three legs, two on the support and one part way down the long handle. A later toaster

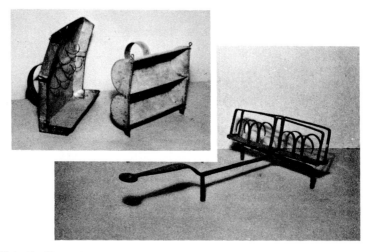

Plate 10. Illustration at left shows tin bird roaster with hooks on which bob whites were roasted, and an apple oven with a capacity of at least eight apples. Other illustration shows a toaster with a revolving head.

has a hinge connecting the handle to the head and the head is in one with the base, standing on four tiny feet.

The waffle iron and the wafer iron were important additions to the utensils. They date far back in history and were used in religious ceremonies as well as serving the home. They are both pincher-shaped contrivances with long handles, the waffle iron having an oblong head and the wafer iron a round head engraved with hearts, a date, hex marks and odd patterns. In old England in 1358 there was a special Sunday set aside in Lent, called Mothering Sunday or Wafering Sunday, when young people were admonished to take a wafer to their mothers. In Sweden it was a waffle

[46]

that was thus used and these wafers and waffles continued to be found in religious ceremonies and made by a village waferer or waffler, for many generations.

Other tools and utensils were at the fireside, such as the kettle-tilter, various spit turners, jack-racks and many forks, skimmers and ladles for handling the meat cooking in the big pots. This work on fireplaces and utensils follows in a second book of the series.

TIN UTENSILS

When tin found its way into the homes there was yet another array of cooking utensils. There was a tin bird roaster and a tin apple roaster. The bird roaster was an upright support holding six hooks, onto which bob whites were hung by their breasts. The bottom part of this small roaster, ten inches wide and eight inches high, was shaped like a pan into which the juices ran. The apple roaster was made with two shelves, holding four apples each. This stood before the fire, resting by one support at its back and two small front feet. The biscuit oven was made in sizes to accommodate the family, large or small. It was in two parts, one hinged to the other, so that the biscuits might be watched as they baked in front of the hot embers. A sheet of tin held the biscuits, resting on supports at the side of the lower part of the oven. Small biscuit ovens were made of one piece, with a narrow ledge at either side, on which rested the pan for the biscuits.

DUTCH OVEN

Every fireplace had the Dutch oven or fire-pan. This was a shallow kettle with three legs, a cover and a hoop handle. The cover had a rim which held the embers when the kettle was placed in the fire. This was a bake oven and was a result of the first principle of putting food directly in the

Plate 11. A tin biscuit oven.

embers to cook. The name Dutch is constantly and errone-ously given to the bake ovens at the side of the fireplace at a later date, but this shallow, twelve-inch kettle with a cover having a rim is the real Dutch oven.

ROASTING

Roasting was done on spits, in every land and clime. A spit was a wooden or an iron skewer which was thrust through the meat to be roasted; the principle of such cook-ing goes back to the beginning of mankind's use of fire. In old England various ways of turning the spit were thought out, from a turnwheel in the wall above the fireplace, turned by a dog shut in the cage, to that of twine which was twisted and which revolved in untwisting, attended to by the chil-dren. The breed of dog that turned the spit in England was called Turnspit, having a long body and short legs, which features lent themselves well to the cage in the wall. In old New England a tin frame was made to hold the spit and to catch the drippings. This was called a roasting kitchen or tin kitchen and stood on legs in front of the fire. The meat was fastened on to the spit by small skewers which fitted into slots in the spit. Revolving the meat as it roasted was accomplished by turning the spit, the pointed handle of which being placed in the notches in the side of the oven.

Inventions followed, giving the busy housewife a mechan- ical device for turning the spit. These were made in the manner of clocks with wheels and pulleys and were attached directly in front of the fire on the mantel above or on an

Plate 12. A tin roasting "kitchen." Upper illustration shows door through which meat could be watched, end of the spit, and the snout out of which the juices were poured. Below is shown method of putting skewers into the spit and a set of the skewers on a hand-wrought holder.

Plate 13. Dutch oven, a shallow iron kettle with three legs and a closely-fitting cover, which was set into and completely covered with the embers. The tin toddy cup shown hung by the chimney or stood on the hearth.

arm at the side of the fireplace opening. This did away with constantly turning the meat as it was roasting.

OVEN IN CHIMNEY

It was not long before an oven for baking was built in the chimney itself. First came the oven at the back of the fire, directly over it or at one side. The oven itself was built with a round floor and a dome-shaped top, like a beehive, so that the heat constantly rotated — a principle learned from the savages. The opening was in the shape of an arch and there was a sill on which rested the wooden door, the first oven door. This was a flat board with an extending handle, put on in such a position that it held the board flat against the opening. A tin door was made in the same manner and both those of wood and of tin are found on the early ovens. It was not until the early 1800's, the period of the development of cast iron, that an iron door was used. This

[50]

Plate 14. Upper illustration shows fireplace with oven at back of chimney. Below is a fireplace with two side ovens, the upper one a bake oven, the lower one an ash oven. Cast iron doors have been substituted for the original wooden doors.

swung on hinges driven into the bricks on the outer edge of the sill. The inner door of wood or of tin continued to be used, making the oven more air-tight. In the first ovens, there were no vents for drafts, the door being left open to create the necessary draft for the fire to burn when the oven was heated. Later plans show there was a draft vent inside the opening, connected with the chimney, which could be adjusted for the proper amount of draw. A plan not often found and which would show that it was not practical was the vent in the floor of the bake oven, lead-ing down to the ash oven below. In such a case, the fire was built in the ash oven and the heat went up into the bake oven, taking with it its attending smoke and smudge. When iron doors were added, the sliding door adjusted the proper amount of air, still passing into the chimney through the vent inside the opening.

The art of baking in these old brick ovens is described in Chapter Five.

SIDE OVENS

Reaching over the fire to the oven in back was a very awkward performance and by another generation the oven was built at the side of the fireplace in line with the opening. A still later change was the building of an ash oven below the bake oven. This was a definite place for the soap ashes. This lower oven did not require a scientific shape and was merely a long, narrow cavity. It seems as if it was a matter of choice about building an ash oven, rather than showing a period of progress. Houses built in the latter part of the nineteenth century have no lower oven while those built a hundred years earlier have two ovens. As long as the ashes were saved, it mattered not whether they were put back into the fire, down a trap door or into an ash oven.

As the fireplace grew smaller and shrank from six feet in length and four feet in depth to that of four feet in length and two feet in depth, so the bake oven was changed. The floor was no longer round but oblong in shape. This resulted in an arched top rather than the dome of the round oven. This oblong oven will be seen in the homes built after the beginning of the eighteenth century. Less wood in the forests near by and less need of baking and cooking in large quantities were the reasons for these changes in the fireplaces and ovens.

WOODEN PANELING

When wooden paneling was used in the kitchens, often a wooden-paneled door, or in some instances two doors, covered both ovens. This was the vogue from the end of the seventeenth century to the end of the eighteenth.

SMOKE OVENS

Almost as necessary as the bake oven was the smoke oven, where meat was hung to smoke as it cooked. This was built in the chimney in one of various places, according to the desire of the owner. It might be in the kitchen at the side of the chimney, on the landing going upstairs, on the cellar stairway, or even up in the attic. Sometimes an oven was built in the attic as a separate oven, connected with the chimney, having an upper part where the meats hung and a lower part in which the fire smoldered. Smoke ovens were often large enough to permit a person to enter and these were called ham rooms. Smoke-houses were frequently built in the yard.

Quite often one finds, in the main chimney, two separate openings, one on one floor and the other above. This shows that the fire was built in the lower opening and that the

Plate 15. Upper illustrations show ovens with wooden paneled doors. Wood or tin was used for the inner door covers. Lower illustrations — At left, very early smoke oven, located in the yard of Old Hadley Museum, Old Hadley, Massachusetts, and built of handmade bricks and shingles. Meat was hung in upper door and fire laid in lower oven. At right, opening high up in the wall back of bake oven, showing chimney and top of oven, Brattleboro, Vermont. Used to heat the room out of the kitchen.

heat went up to the meats in the upper oven. The lower oven has a floor for the fire or firepot and there is a flue connecting directly into the upper chamber. The upper opening has hooks on the side wall or poles extended from wall to wall to hold the meat hooks. The openings for the meat are sometimes of great size for it has been learned that whole, dressed hogs were roasted at one time as well as small portions of meat. Smoked meat was kept in bins of oats and even packed in charcoal, which method preserved it for many months.

Corn cobs and hickory bark were used in making the smudge for smoking the meat. The fuel smoldered without burning briskly, and a fresh fire was made each day for three successive days, the length of time it took the meat to cook. A small wooden sled has been found on which the meat was placed, used instead of hooks. But this charred so quickly that the trouble of making new sleds soon proved that hooks were more practical.

The construction of the fireplaces and ovens shows the approximate period in which a house was built. Changes in living conditions, coming toward the end of the nine-teenth century, necessitated changes in heating and cooking, and the old ovens disappeared. By searching for old lines of molding, for replaced bricks or for sealed-up openings, the original positions can often be found and restored. Much has been destroyed, however, which can not be replaced. Private individuals, societies and museums are endeavoring to preserve the old homes and the old fireplaces, in such a way that they will remain standing for many generations to come.

CONTENTS OF KITCHENS

Little is known of the contents of that one-room struc-ture of 1620. Benches, stools and chair-forms were the first attempt at furniture. The ships coming from England were more concerned in bringing foodstuffs, household implements, tools and clothing; only a chest or two filled with such things actually came over on the *Mayflower*. A few decades later the homes boasted several rooms and a loft, and the kitchen then had tables and chairs, a dresser or pine cupboard, and a turn-up bed, or a four-poster bed under which rolled the trundle bed. As the ships continued to bring families to the new land, many of the family heirlooms in furniture came with them. Carpenters, coopers, and mechanics of all trades came with those ships and they set about their work here. That crowded kitchen of long ago contained also the butter churn, the loom, the cheese-press and all the pantry tools. The kitchen was the one room in those first years that had heat, coming from the big fireplace, and that fact explains the reason for the concentration of so much activity in so small a space.

EATING CUSTOMS

The eating customs of one hundred and more years ago are revealed in a collection of wooden ware. Primitive man and savages used stones as tables, chairs and utensils, and the progress up to the time of the linen, glass and silver of our beautiful dining tables was a slow one. In the old country at one time, thought to be typical of Russia, the table was a thick, oaken plank, supported by trestles, and in this were hollows, serving each person as a bowl. The plank was washed after each meal and stood on end against the wall. In this country the settlers had a similar oaken plank but without hollows, standing on trestles; and they too washed it and stood it on end when the meal was over. The family sat on one side only. This arrangement provided more space in the all-too-crowded room. The expression, "The boards fairly groaned with food," came from the use of these large, thick, oaken planks.

The hutch table was another natural invention for those early kitchens. This was a combination of table, settle and chest. Built like a settle with a storage box for a seat, the wide back could be dropped down and resting on the arms made a table. The word "hutch" means a place in which to store, such as grain hutch, rabbit hutch and the like, and the box seat of the combination table and settle provided space for bed clothing or such household equipment.

Benches and chair-forms served as chairs and it is said that children stood behind their elders throughout the meal. Sitting at a table to eat, however, was not always the customary procedure. The early Puritans often stood and ate from the pots and kettles with their fingers, drinking from noggins and gourds.

EATING UTENSILS

Inventories and letters show that wooden plates (called trenchers), platters, dishes (probably bowls), and spoons were brought from England. Then the handyman of the house set about making more of an assortment for the table. The trenchers were both round and square, and without doubt the square ones came from England. These had a round indentation in one corner where salt was placed for seasoning. Also from England came the custom of using the under side of the trencher for a second course. A few plates in my collection show marks on the back side, and "up country" they speak of "the dinner side and the pie side." One large trencher illustrated, labeled by a descendant, is said to have been used in "1740 or earlier." There is a nick in the rim where it rested on the shelf for more than a generation. Unfortunately the owner's name, stamped on the rim, cannot be deciphered. Plates range from a tiny one five inches in diameter to those of fourteen inches. These are

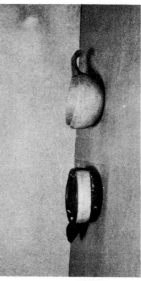

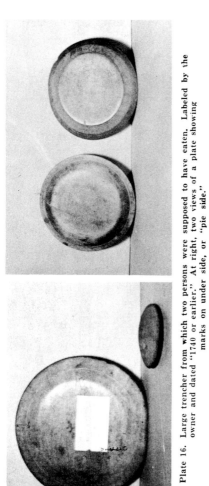

Plate 16. Large trencher from which two persons were supposed to have eaten. Labeled by the owner and dated "1740 or earlier." At right, two views of a plate showing marks on under side, or "pie side."

Plate 17. Small individual eating bowls and two drinking cups, one at left labeled as being "very old."

[58]

Plate 18. Large Shaker eating bowl with copper handles.

seldom round for, as has been explained, the mandrel lathe did not hold the wood securely. As wood also shrinks with age, sidewise and with the grain, this fact, too, made the plates more oval than round.

New England thrift compelled two people to eat from the same trencher. The story goes that one deacon of a church made a trencher for each member of his family and was reproved for his extravagance. If a boy and a girl ate together in the same trencher they were considered engaged.

Stews, vegetables and porridge made up the main dish and these were served in a central bowl. From this, each one helped himself by dipping out with his own bowl or by using a wooden ladle or gourd. Spoons with which to eat are not easily found. Such an unimportant thing as a small spoon was counted of no value when it became worn, and collectors are always wary of thinking that the spoons which exist can be truly old. Weathered and used, any spoon might pass for an old one. Forks were a long time coming into use, and with ten fingers and a spoon there was little need of worrying about how to pass the food from the bowl to the mouth. Hooking the little finger and the thumb together left the three fingers flat as a scoop.

[59]

Salt bowls stood on the table as they do today. They were large affairs and indicated a dividing line between the guests and those of common rank. They are of many interesting shapes; and the one unfailing earmark is the glistening of the salt. Individual salts must have come later when more thought was given to manners, but the family salt bowl was six or more inches in diameter. Salt came to the home in coarse form and was crushed in the mortar with the pestle.

Plate 19. An assembly of salt bowls.

Boxes for the salt stood on the shelf over the fireplace, or often a brick was removed to make a niche in which the box might be kept.

THE NOGGIN AND THE TANKARD

The wooden pitcher, which was passed from mouth to mouth, was called a noggin. Noggin has two derivations: one meaning a block of wood, and the other meaning the measure of half a cup. The wooden pitcher could well be called either, for it was made by hand from a block of wood and it was made in exact measurements of one, two, three, or four cups. An unusual set of three noggins is illustrated,

Plate 20. Noggins. Three at right hold two, four and six cups respectively.

showing hand cutting in pentagon shape. Ordinarily, noggins were turned on a lathe and were round.

The tankard was another drinking vessel as was the noggin. It was staved and hooped and had a cover. Rarely was it made without a cover. It held the toddy and was kept near the fireplace. A tankard was not used at the table, but only for hospitality by the fire. An unusual one is pictured which has a hole through which the toddy stick was thrust to heat the toddy (Plate 22).

OTHER UTENSILS

Made like the tankard is the little syrup jug. It stands eight inches high. One of the staves was cut in the shape of a lip, over which the cover fits. The staves are pointed at the bottom so that the edges might catch on the table and the jug would not slide off.

Such things as spoon holders, individual egg cups and sugar bowls of wood gradually found their way to the table. The sugar bowls (Plate 21) were for brown sugar, the sugar that came from the maple tree, and white sugar, the latter a great luxury. These sugar bowls are found in many sizes, from that of four inches to one of fifteen inches. The spoon holder is a lovely thing — a hollowed piece of poplar with a round bottom pegged in. Small wooden butter knives are trivial things, but one can well visualize the need of them when butter was used at the table.

Shown in an illustration (Plate 6) is a very rare Indian eating scoop. It came from the Gay Head Indian tribe of

Plate 21. Sugar bowls, said to be from Pennsylvania. Wire handle added at a later date. At right, spoon holder with spoons and butter knife.

Martha's Vineyard. It was cut to fit the hand and on the handle is an inscription which has been interpreted as indicating that it was made by one of low rank for one of high rank. There are teeth marks on one edge, showing how the food was conveyed directly to the mouth. It is just what the name implies — an eating scoop.

Wooden table ware was not used exclusively in those early homes. The well-to-do families had china and pewter, brought or sent from across the water. The houses and furnishings of the families of wealth and nobility were in keeping with their finer ways of living. In such homes the wooden table ware would be found only in the servants' quarters and the kitchens. In the homes of the middle class

[62]

and of those living in the rural sections wooden ware was the general thing — the "best" dishes of china and pewter lying in the cupboards and dressers waiting for "company."

When families moved on to new, unexplored land they seldom carried with them china and pewter, but wooden utensils. A few heirlooms might be sacredly cherished on those journeys but there were too many hardships to consider sentiment. There is a pie crimper up in New Hampshire that took the journey in a covered wagon to Texas. It came back with the next generation along with a yard-square piece of chintz that had hung in those first windows of the bride. An unusual butter paddle in the collection went on a similar journey to Ohio and made a return trip — only

Plate 22. Syrup jug and tankard.

in this case the owner sold it, whereas the pie crimper could never be bought.

Breaking new ground in those distant lands meant mak-

[63]

ing more wooden ware — wooden dishes for the table and wooden utensils and implements for the home. This migrating continued into the nineteenth century. It was then that factories were supplying china and glass in greater quantities and wooden table ware was used only in outlying sections, those too far away to have access to "modern" utensils. Even in the present day, one can find in the remote sections of the South and West wooden ware on the tables. Assisting me at one of my lectures were two colored men from the South. They were delighted to see the old wooden dishes and, with unrestrained joy, they showed how they passed around the noggin and how they ate with their fingers from plates and bowls.

THE PANTRY

When the families began to prosper — "feel their oats," as was the common expression — the houses were built with better accommodations. In the course of time there was a pantry, a "butt'ry," a milk room, a shed, a shed chamber and an attic. The appearance of these homes came at the end of the eighteenth century but it was not for another hundred years that it was a general thing to see a well-planned home.

The pantry was added to the one-room house as the first necessity, and every kitchen had its pantry, whether it was large or small. In that space was the sink, made either of soapstone, stone or wood. The water was brought in from the outside pump or spring, and the outlet was a pipe running from the sink through a hole in the window or wall. If possible, a spring was piped into the sink, and the water flowed incessantly. There was one large window for light and air. Shelves were built on three sides of the room, some enclosed at the lower part and some with cupboards in the upper part. Very often there was a large shelf near the window used as a work table.

In the cupboard underneath the shelves were the wooden bowls, the milk pans, earthen crocks, jars and pitchers. On the shelves above stood the baking dishes of tin and earthenware, baking ingredients and odd boxes of all sizes. Spices, small quantities of sugar, meals and powdered herbs were kept in the round and oval boxes. Tin boxes and wooden boxes held the sets of spices, each small box marked with the name of the spice.

By the sink hung the ladles and dippers, with long handles and short handles, and of all shapes and sizes. Gourds were often used, as they were easily made — also easily destroyed. The pantry tools were at hand, either hanging or in drawers — such as the rolling pin, chopping knife, scoops, mashers, spatulas, lemon squeezer, pie crimper, apple parer. A mortar and pestle stood on the top shelf and a bucket or two stood under the sink for water from the well. What an endless task both utensils had — the mortar was always in use and the never-ceasing supply of water wore out the wooden buckets!

THE ''BUTT'RY''

The buttery (or "butt'ry," as it was more commonly called) served as an overflow of the pantry. Originally this room was used as a storeroom for wines and liquors and other provisions, but eventually it held everything in general. Here, in the old homes, were found the large utensils — sap buckets and tubs when not in use, butter boxes and butter tubs, the molasses keg holding three gallons, the rum kegs, and water kegs, the sugar bucket, the dye tub when not filled with dye and standing on the hearth, the soft soap barrel, the meal barrels and the salt tubs, not forgetting the

[65]

powdering tub which was used in "salting down" the meats.

The meals were corn, rye, barley and wheat and, at a later time, oatmeal. The grains were winnowed in the large sieves of splint, ground between stones at the mill, and sifted in fine horse-hair sieves for use in the home. There was a canal flour, often called middlings, which was the second sifting of the meal and much coarser. In the barrel of corn meal was a rock, the size of a pumpkin, placed there to keep the meal from lying heavily together. The salt in the "butt'ry" was the rock salt that came in crystal form; two grades of it, one for the cattle and one for the table. The latter was whiter and cleaner.

The "butt'ry" was planned much as was the pantry, with a large window and many shelves, and both "butt'ry" and pantry were like good-sized rooms in well-to-do homes.

THE MILK ROOM

A third room in the house of the well-to-do family was the milk room. Here were found the butter churn, the cheese-press, the racks for the buckets, and the cheese closet. This cheese closet was an open cupboard of three or four shelves with a frame for the door. Over the frame was tacked cheesecloth to let in the air and keep out the dust and the cheese fly. This meshed cloth derives its name from its use on the cheese closet. The milk room removed from the kitchen the almost daily work of making the butter and cheese, thus saving much fuss in that busy room. However, if the family was small or poor the kitchen and pantry had to serve the purpose of the other two rooms, the "butt'ry" and the milk room.

THE PINE CUPBOARD

There was rarely a kitchen that did not have a pine cupboard. These cupboards were fashioned after the Welsh dresser, having open shelves above and cupboards below, and which was brought from across the water. The early New England cupboards, patterned after these, were more severe in style however. Later ones had doors on both the upper and lower parts, enclosing the shelves, and sometimes drawers were put in between these two compartments with a projecting shelf which served as a place on which to work. Such a cupboard held the things which did not belong in the pantry, such as the everyday dishes of glass, wood, pewter and earthenware, the tea and coffee pots, the tea cannister, and the knives, forks and spoons for the table.

The cooking and preparing of meals was done on the long tavern tables in the middle of the room or on the table shelf in the pantry. The spinning-wheel and the flax wheel stood in the corner, ready for their never-ending work, and a loom was often crowded into this same busy kitchen. From dawn until dark, and then by the light of candles, the women folk spent their days with such labor as would now seem almost impossible.

THE SHED CHAMBER AND THE ATTIC

The small room over the shed was called the shed chamber and it must have been a most interesting place. Here hung strings of dried apples, dried herbs, and corn shucks ready for braiding into mats; here were stored the winter supply of vegetables, tubs of maple sugar cakes, odd boxes and trunks of varied shapes and sizes; and under the eaves was a low four-poster bed. It was a real storeroom and overflow of the kitchen.

And there was the attic which was reached by narrow stairs, scarcely wide enough for one's foot. The big chimney took a goodly amount of space in the middle of the room and light came from two small windows at either end. Here hung herbs and the traced corn that could not find a place in the shed chamber. Here, too, was bedding, pillows and feather beds suspended from clotheslines, furniture, chests and trunks that had accumulated, often from generation to generation. Sentiment and thrift were too strong charac- teristics of the old New England families, and little was ever thrown away. The old attics hold more memories, too, than any other part of the homes.

Plate. 22a. Two candle dippers taken off their frame. Each dipper averaged 36 hooks from which hung the nine-inch-long twisted wick of tow. The arms of the frame holding the dippers swung around as the wicks were dipped to facilitate the work.

CHAPTER FIVE

Pantry Tools and Labor-Saving Devices — Products of the Handy Man with an Inventive Mind

A N ARRAY of pantry tools in a collection of kitchen wooden ware expresses the humble, daily duties of past generations. The creative ability of our ancestors never ceases to be a wonder to a collector of the early implements and tools. These industrious people fashioned for themselves the things to be produced later by machinery, and the construction of their hand work is perfect and complete in every detail.

Pantry tools as a whole are placed in a period of from seventy-five to one hundred and fifty years ago. Beginning about 1850, factories were turning out these products. Unless a direct descendant of a family owning these tools can estimate their age, there is little chance that a connoisseur of wooden pieces can tell how long a tool has been in use. Some bear a date, scratched on them, but most of them may be classified merely by the kind of labor they performed — either early hand labor or later machine labor.

METHODS OF PREPARING APPLES

Apples supplied the table in many ways. There were pies made from dried, sliced apples, the apple butter and apple sauce, the many barrels of cider for drinking and the vinegar for cooking. To pare three hundred bushels of apples was a common occurrence, and this need brought about the apple-paring bees, which usually turned into occasions of festivity. Whether it was raising a barn or making a quilt or paring apples, many hands made light work and gave the old days their social times.

The first paring machines show great ingenuity. There is

Plate 23. Apple parers. One is mounted on a bench on which operator sat. The others were used on a table, one at right attached to table by wooden screw.

one on the end of a four-legged bench, having a blade on the end of a free-working arm, prongs and a crank. It would seem at first thought that a lazy man had contrived to do the work without over-exertion. One that screwed on to the table is pictured also. It is a very beautiful thing. Many were built on boards, with cogwheels and belts rigged up to turn the arm that held the apple; these could be placed on a table or held in the lap. Wooden parers were used for many years until the patented machines of iron took their place. Those of iron eventually cored as well as pared. The first parer was patented in 1803 by Moses Coats, a mechanic of Downingtown, Pennsylvania, but wooden parers continued to be used well into the nineteenth century.

After the apples were pared, there were two different

[70]

ways of cutting them for dried apples. One way was to quarter them, remove the core and then string them on a heavy thread two yards long with a big needle. Such strings were draped over racks or hooks to dry. The other way was to core the apple and then slice it. These slices were placed on apple driers, and here again each man made his own. One of splint is a long basket, two feet wide and shallow, with a flat handle of wound splint. The creator made a mistake when he did not put two hickory bands at the edge for support as the splint is giving way in places. The basket (Plate 126) came from a home in New Hampshire, and the story of it was told to me by the owner himself as he pared an apple and explained, munching the pieces when he had finished. He was the last of his family and was living in a fine old house into which, unfortunately, we were not invited to enter. The slices of apples were placed in the basket and the basket placed on the window sill, half outside and half inside, and the window was shut down on it to hold it. When one half was dried, the other half was turned outside, and the basket was rotated until all the slices had the sunshine. The dried apples were then strung or left loose, packed in boxes and put away for the winter. A bushel of apples made seven pounds of dried apples, and these not only supplied the family but were often taken to town and exchanged for necessary commodities.

Up the road "a piece" was found another drier, but one of a later date. This consisted of a large oblong frame to which were nailed narrow slats. The slices were laid on this frame and it was taken out-of-doors and placed on sawhorses. No particular skill was needed in making this box-like frame.

When the sliced apples were dried in the house, a similar rack with a frame and slats was used. Four long hooks were screwed in the rafters over the hearth, at points making an oblong shape, two feet by four feet. Two sticks were placed on the end hooks, one at either end. On these sticks, the drier, filled with sliced apples, rested and the heat from the open fire dried the slices. These hooks are often seen in the old kitchens today.

A cobweb drier is shown in Plate 125. This was sus-

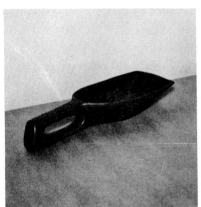

Plate 24. A Shaker apple-butter scoop, and two-way scoops — one end for stirring, the other for scooping.

pended from the center and the heat spun it around as the slices dried, all of which was more romantic than sanitary.

SHAKER APPLE PRODUCTS

The Shakers were known as much for their apple products as for their other industries. The *Community Industries of the Shakers* says that the sisters trimmed and cored the apples while the brethren ran the paring machines. This was in the beginning of the nineteenth century, and apple sauce, dried apples and apple butter were made then and sold in large quantities. The Shakers had a drying house in which there was a stove on the ground floor, furnishing heat,

[72]

and on the floor above there were large bins to hold the sliced apples, which were stirred as they dried. The dried apples were kept in barrels until they were needed. Since the modern theory of sunshine and vitamins would advocate the out-of-doors drying racks, the Shaker method was not an improvement over the old way.

In the collection there is a Shaker apple-butter scoop which measures eighteen inches long and eight inches wide and has a handle with two arms and a crossbar — all cut from one piece of wood. It was used standing on end, one hand holding an arm and the other resting and pressing on the crosspiece. The thin edge of the scoop kept the apple butter, or sauce as it might be, from sticking to the bottom of the kettle. Huge copper kettles, measuring two and three feet across, were used in making the butter. The Shakers had buckets for the purpose of holding the apple butter. The bucket had iron bands and a cover that set in with an inside edge, and quite often the bucket was painted red.

A newcomer to the collection is the Pennsylvania apple-butter stirrer, with a handle 9 feet long. This had a companion stirrer with a five-foot handle. The head is paddle-shape, two feet in length, full of holes bored with an augur. Used in the huge copper kettles — iron turned the apples black — the apple butter flowed in and out of the holes as the paddle was pulled back and forth. The long handle enabled the worker to stand away from the intense heat of the fire. Showing where the paddle rested on the edge of the kettle, there is a worn groove about two feet from the head. This would give a rough estimate of the diameter of the kettle, multiplying that distance by two.

APPLES FOR EATING AND FOR DRINK

An old rule for apple butter reads: "10 gallons sweet cider, 3 pecks of cored and quartered apples — do a few at

Plate 25. This cider-press rack was also used as an apple-drying rack.

a time — cook slowly. Add 10 pounds of sugar, 5 ounces of cinnamon. Stir for 5, 6 or more hours with a wooden paddle." It sounds good to us of today. If apples were scarce, pumpkins were used.

Apple sauce was flavored with molasses, apple molasses, maple sugar molasses or cider. A "two-way" scoop is pictured (Plate 24), one end a thin blade for stirring the sauce, the other for scooping it up. But it could not be guaranteed that the liquid would not run down on the hand as the stirrer was tipped and the scoop used.

Cider was the common drink of all the early colonies, and bequeathing barrels of cider in wills was as common as leaving furniture or household supplies. Every family made its own cider, as apples were plentiful. Cider was used at the table and also taken to the fields in kegs, for apparently water was not healthful in those days of little sanitation.

*Correspondence from New Jersey gives a graphic pic-

*N. R. Ewan, Curator Camden County Historical Society, New Jersey.

ture of the old method of making cider. The writer describes the old hand method and that by power.

Apple pomace was laid on a wooden, slatted rack with layers of straw as a binder in between the layers of pomace. This was called a "cheese" when all set up. As the wooden screw pressed down on the "cheese," the juice was forced out while at the same time the pomace was squeezed out of the mass at the sides. This was cut down with a knife called a "cutting down" knife, having a long, thin blade in an inverted position, on a short handle. The pomace was placed back on the top of the mass and another pressing took place. This was done two or three times, according to the amount of juice left in the pomace. The cider trickled out into buckets below the rack and the buckets were emptied into barrels. A bucket funnel was used, the size of an ordinary bucket, with a wooden funnel.

A power press was a different story. Coming in the time of inventions, it pressed by power the pomace which had been put into cotton bags, with a rack laid between each bag, ten or twelve bags being the proper height for the "knuckle joint" press. Each bag contained the equivalent of 10 bushels of apples in pomace form and the large presses produced about 400 gallons of cider, made from approximately 100 bushels of fruit. The ancient hand press produced about 2 gallons of cider to a bushel of apples.

The correspondent tells of the press in Bucks County Historical Museum, at Doylestown, Pennsylvania, stating that it was so large it had to be placed in position before the building was built and its age is estimated at 200 years.

After the cider was poured into barrels, the head was sealed. Near the bottom of the barrel was a bunghole and in the early days this was sealed with a cluster of straw. This made a stopper and the straw was so deftly twisted it

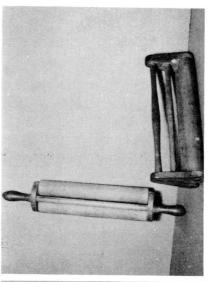

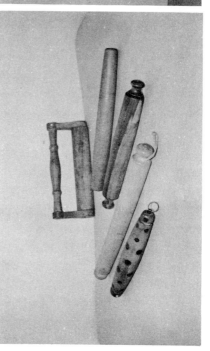

Plate 26. Various types of rolling pins. The dark one at right is of lignum-vitæ; the one at lower left has mahogany inserts. The two grooved ones are cooky rollers.

was not only air tight and moisture tight but kept out all insects.

The drinks contained spirits quite generally, which made for much intoxication. Rum was brought back on whaling vessels and it was in 1745 that an Admiral Vernon was the first to dilute the rum for the sailors. Grog was a mixture of spirits and water, and unsweetened. Toddy had less spirits than grog and was sweetened and served hot, stirred with toddy sticks. Flip was cider with spirits added, lemon and sugar put in to suit the taste. Flip was stirred with an iron flip dog also called a loggerhead.

Vinegar was made from the inferior apples. Thus an orchard of apples provided raw fruit, apple butter and apple sauce, cider for drinking, and vinegar for cooking and preserving.

PIES AND COOKIES

Rolling pins, seventy-five and one hundred years old, make an odd array in a collection of wooden ware. The first rolling-pin was what the name implied — a pin that rolled. It had no handle, only tapering ends which were left on when the pin was made on the lathe; thus it was higher in the middle than at the ends. A later pin had one handle; the pin could be steadied with one hand while the other pushed it over the dough. Then came the rolling-pins of many sizes and styles, from that two inches long for a child to those twenty inches long and five inches in diameter. Maple was the common wood used, but one is of beech, one of cherry, and those made on the whaling vessels were made of lignum-vitæ. Handles were short and chubby or long and thin. Two rollers in a frame set with two rods above for a handle is an odd rolling-pin — so odd, in fact, that a dealer called it a wringer for clothes and was not impressed with the idea that it might be a rare rolling-pin. From seaport towns came others of the same style made of ivory or bone. Somewhat similar is the one roller set in a frame, but this is less easily balanced when it is used. A fancy rolling-pin is the one that has graded circular inlays of mahogany, twenty-three in all, the larger ones being in the center and the smaller ones at the nub handle. This was a creation thought out on board a whaling vessel.

The cooky roller has corrugated grooves and was also made in many sizes, the smallest ones measuring three inches. Other elaborately-cut rollers were for making hardtack, called "sea bread," a coarse, flat cake made of flour and water and used on board whaling vessels. The cakes were flattened thin and rolled once with the roller which left deep indentations. Two such rollers are in the collection, one of unusual beauty and one coming from the whaling vessel on which the lignum-vitæ chopping bowl (shown in Plate 72e) was made. This was cut in a waffle pattern and done so crudely, the pattern did not come to an even finish.

The meat pounder with a corrugated head and a handle has been used for rolling cookies. The distinction between the pounder and the roller would be in the shape of the head. That for the meat has a tapering head, larger at the end, while the one for the cookies has corrugations of the same size the whole length of the head. To make cookies, the dough was rolled to a thickness of about half an inch and put into a pan. It was then rolled with the roller to make the corrugations. When the cake was done, it was cut into oblong pieces, making thick cookies. One such cooky of molasses is in the collection, having been made just before the roller was sold.

There are cooky prints which have been confused with butter prints. Those for butter have a handle, made in one piece, while those for cookies are flat, circular discs, often having a pattern on both sides. They are commonly used in Pennsylvania and New York state.

In Pennsylvania, marzipan or marchpane cakes were made as early as 1563 for the Christmas tree to be eaten before Twelfthnight. The molds for the cakes were oblong in shape, 2 by 3 inches and 5 by 8 inches, being ¾ inches deep

Plate 27. Cooky rollers; sometimes used as meat pounders.

with the print or stamp at the bottom. The wood used for the molds was boxwood, pear, cherry, apple, maple, walnut or pine and the patterns were figures, birds, animals and flowers.

The batter for the cookies was made of almond meal or paste, from chopped kernels of apricot stones, wheat flour or fine cornmeal, honey or sugar syrup or sometimes with cider brandy or wine. The dough was rolled thin and pressed into the molds. Then they were cut around the edge with a pastry jigger which was an early cut brass tool. Some jiggers had one wheel at one end, others had two wheels, while the opposite end curved and was used as in "pinking." Besides the patterned molds, there were round molds not unlike those used in printing butter. These molds have a decided hand-made appearance and often have a pattern on either side. The cakes were covered with frosting of vegetable juices of colors suitable to the design, showing individual creative ability.

Gingerbread prints are similar to the oblong cooky prints, although they might be larger. Some have one single pattern while others have patterns for each small section, if the print was used for a cake which was to be broken into sections — similar to maple sugar molds. The prints were pressed on to the dough after it had been spread in the pan.

The table of our ancestors would not have been properly supplied without pies. It is hard to state when pies first appeared, but they must have been made when more thought could be given to the variety of food than in those more difficult days. The meat pie came first, used as a main dish, and the making of mince pies followed. The content of those mince pies was as interesting as the contents of a boy's first pocket! When meat from the farm animals was not obtainable, bear meat was a good substitute. Added to this were syrups and meat juices for liquids, dried fruit, and nuts, the whole highly seasoned with spices. Who could imagine a more wonderful feast! Pies made from fruits, squash and pumpkins came in due time, and the pantry boasted of a continual row of pies. At Thanksgiving time many more pies were made than were to be used and these were put away to "freeze" for the meals to come. They were called frozen pies and were stacked one on the other in the larder, sometimes as many as fifty.

A pie crimper was used when putting two crusts together. They were ordinarily of wood, but often the family boasted of a bone crimper, made on a returning whaling vessel. One crimper of wood has four points at the end opposite the wheel, used to prick air holes in the crust. This crimper has a pewter pin holding the wheel into place. It shows more hand work in its carving than New England could boast of. Crimpers of wood and tin or of all metal followed.

A pie peel (Plate 9) was a kitchen necessity in the days of brick ovens, to hold the pies as they were slid in or taken out. The pie peel had a short handle, whereas the bread peel had a long handle.

The pie lifter was a more recent pantry acquisition. It has a short handle, and two wires held the pie as it was taken to or from the oven. It resembles a small pitch fork.

FROM CORN TO HASTY PUDDING

If it had not been for the Indian corn, history of the New England colonies might have read differently. A plague had killed a tribe of Indians in the section in which the Pilgrims first located. It was a custom of the Indians to bury their dead with food and utensils that the departing souls might have food and means of preparing it as they made their journey into the other worlds. Thus it came about that the

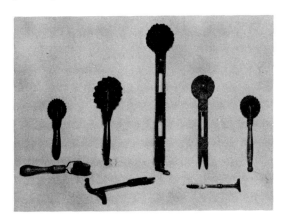

Plate 28. An array of pie crimpers. The second from right has points for pricking the crust and a pewter pin for wheel. In front are two pastry jiggers.

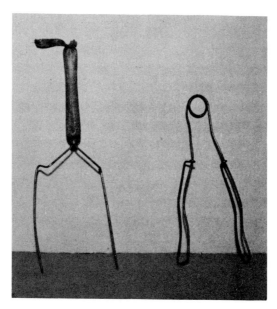

Plate 29. Pie lifters.

Pilgrims found these mounds of corn with a few iron utensils. The corn supplied what little food was available in
that first winter, along with fish from the sea, birds from the
air and wild animals. Planting was begun in that first spring
of 1621 but it was a scant harvest that was reaped in the
fall. Many seasons came and went before there was an
abundance. This history is given fully by George F. Wil-
lison in his *Saints and Strangers*.

The best ears of corn were set aside for seed for the following year, when the corn ripened at the harvest. The
husks of these ears were turned back and braided, which was
called tracing and the ears were tied together and hung up
to dry — in the shed, the upper chamber or in the attic.

SHELLING CORN

The job of shelling the corn often fell to the lot of the
young boys. The most primitive way of shelling was to place

a shovel or an iron ash peel on a tub and scrape the corn across the edge. The kernels fell into a bucket. The bucket pictured (Plate 118) marked "Corn," doubtless held these kernels until they were used for grinding or for popping. A shelling tub, however, provided a quicker way as a larger number of ears could be shelled in it at one time. This tub was a tree trunk, probably the sour gum tree, measuring fully three feet high and two or three feet across. It was hollowed out and a bottom was constructed in one of two

Plate 30. Two views of a corn sheller made from the trunk of a tree. The bottom, a thick plank in which holes were bored, is held in place by wooden pegs driven through trunk. At right is shown a three foot long pestle used in a trunk corn sheller. This type of pestle was also used in making sauerkraut.

Plate 31. A corn sheller at the Rufus Putnam House, Rutland, Mass., showing standard and trough.

ways. The easier way was to set in, a few inches from the ground, a board in which many holes had been bored. The second way was to drive rods through holes bored in the base of the trunk. Either way formed a grating through which the kernels fell. The tub was partly filled with ears, and a hickory sapling, or a heavy ash pestle, was used to pound off the kernels. A shelling tub made in this fashion, with a grating of rods, is in the Wayside Inn, Sudbury, Massachusetts. A picture (Plate 30) is shown of one with a board floor, now in the collection. Corn was ground in mortars and later at grist mills, and the grain was kept in bins. A pair of palette paddles are shown with which the grain was taken out, a paddle in each hand, used primarily in grist mills. These were also called bolting boards (Plate 37).

A hand sheller was made from two thick planks, each about a foot long and eight inches wide, one made concave

[84]

and the other rounded. Both planks have a shaped end with a hole through which a peg was driven to fasten the two parts together. One plank has a handle set in at the opposite end. Nails were driven in all over the inside of both planks and the heads cut off so that the stubs might act as a grater. The rounded plank with no handle was fastened on to an easel and the other plank, pegged to it, rubbed the ear of corn across the nail stubs. The kernels fell down a trough into a tub. One such sheller is in the collection, a very early piece with its first red paint, but the one pictured on a frame is in the Rufus Putnam Memorial House in Rutland, Massachusetts.

The husking pin was a sharpened peg three or four inches long which had a strap that fitted over the thumb and was used for husking the ears.

The corn cobs were saved for burning with hickory bark when meat was to be smoked.

THE INDIANS' SAMP

The Indians first parboiled their corn in hot water and then ground the kernels in a mortar of stone with a stone pestle. The meal was coarse when sifted and when cooked with water made a sort of hominy which the Indians called *samp*. The settlers soon learned how to do this. The mor-

Plate 32. This corn sheller from the collection was fastened to an easel.

tar which they used was a slender tree trunk about three feet high, hollowed out to a depth of only nine or ten inches. The pestle was a long, chubby-shaped stone or an L-shaped one of wood, cut from the tree at the joining of a limb, which gave a hammer shape. Such a mortar is pictured (Plate 74) and it will never be known whether it was used by the Indians or the white men. It is shaped like a tall urn and shows the marks of the knife which fashioned it.

The hasty pudding spoon and sticks are pictured (Plate 33). The spoon shows a snubbed end from being used upright, and the handle has a peculiar angle to give a better leverage. Hasty pudding sticks had long handles and a short head, as the kettle stood on the hearth and the pudding was stirred from a standing position. The young folks often took turns stirring and the name "hasty" belies the long job. Mush, corn meal pudding and Indian pudding were the names it went by, and more often than not it was eaten twice a day.

The Indians made cakes of cornmeal and water and baked them in a fire hole, in hot ashes. These acquired the name of "ash cakes" and when the white man baked them in the embers in his fireplace, they were still called ash cakes. The settlers in the South baked similar cakes on the iron head of a hoe, the handle protruding into the room. This, to the busy housewife, was a most suitable utensil and thus gave the cakes the name of "hoe cakes." This might have been done in the North, but a wooden slab, a foot long and eight inches wide, with a protruding handle put on in the manner of a prop served as baking equipment. The board was called a "bannock" board and the cakes were called "bannock cakes." Thus one sees how each group of people and in fact each generation produced things in the daily life and gave to them different names, some to be passed down to other generations and some to be forgotten.

Brown bread was made of corn meal and rye, mixed with water and baked in the brick oven or in the Dutch oven in the embers. A finer bread, fit "for the minister when he called" was made by using corn meal, rye meal, yeast and water. Bread with leaven or yeast is first found

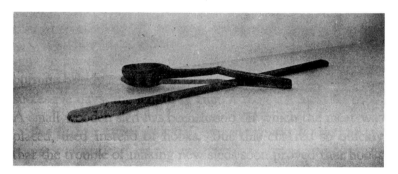

Plate 33. Hasty pudding spoon and stirrer.

in history among the Egyptians. The Bible records that Moses used leaven. The art was passed to the Greeks and Romans and thence down to other peoples.

Next to corn meal puddings, bread was the mainstay of the family. Yeast was kept in earthen jars and handed down from one generation to another. The first batch was made from hops, froth of mash or beer settlings, boiled down with potatoes. Another rule was 1 pound flour, 1/4 pound brown sugar, salt, 2 gallons water: boil one hour and bottle when warm. In New England it was "emptins" and in Pennsylvania it was "sots." Sometimes yeast cakes were made by mixing the liquid with corn meal and rolling the mixture flat. Each new batch of yeast had some of the old taken as a foundation and if the old did by chance run out, another lot could be borrowed of a neighbor.

The bread trough originally was a hollowed-out log, but

as time went on the trough was made from boards in an oblong shape with mitered or dove-tailed ends. A cover set in and rested on the sides which slant toward the bottom. Some troughs were made as a table by adding legs to the bottom, a handy arrangement.

Trough was pronounced like *trow* in some localities and "bread tray" was as much used as "bread trough." Bread was often made in the common round wooden bowls and some families resorted to large tubs for their batch of dough (Plate 110).

In the four-sided trough there are square notches at either end, an inch or more from the top. In these lay the stick on which the sieve rested as the flour was sifted into the dough mixture. This stick has been called a temse, but research brings up the name of lintel and templet. Webster says that temse means to *sift*. A lintel "holds up a mantel, door or window, and is a stick, log or stone slab." Templet is from the Latin word *templum,* meaning "a short piece of timber, iron or stone, placed in a wall under a girder or other beam, to distribute the weight of pressure." Thus this stick in the bread trough held up the sifter and was properly called a lintel or a templet. One of the sayings lasting these many years is "to set the Thames on fire." This has come from the word temse, meaning that the friction of the sieve on the temse or lintel would set the stick afire.

In the three-hundred-year-old Fairbanks Homestead in Dedham, Massachusetts, there is a bread trough with the original lintel. One day an elderly lady, attended by members of her family, visited the house, and on seeing the lintel she began to recite a poem about the "lintel in the bread trough." Before the curator could find his way to her to ask her about the poem, the crowd pressed her on. Searching the pages of old literature has not yet brought the poem to light. There is now in the collection a bread trough with a lintel in it, a rare piece for a collector.

A flour scoop in the shape of a shell was long used for flour and the pores of the wood are well filled with the soft dust. There is also a paddle that was used to stir the bread, and a long wooden knife to cut the dough into loaves. All three pieces show particles of flour in the wood.

The bread peel is the long-handled wooden shovel with which the loaves were placed in the oven and taken out again. They measure as much as five feet long, for the first ovens were built in the chimney back of the fire. The peel was sprinkled with corn meal and the loaves placed on it, two at a time, and shoved into the oven. With a quick snap of the wrist the peel was pulled back, leaving the loaves on the bricks or on cabbage or oak leaves. In the same manner a quick push put the peel under the loaves when they were ready to be taken out. It was considered an omen of good luck to give a bread peel to a bride. Pennsylvania women were called good bread makers, but Ohio claimed to have the best bread makers.

BAKING BREAD

The art of baking in the old brick ovens is all but forgotten in these modern days. A fire was made in the oven, a fire quite likely of birch which was a slow-burning wood and gave great heat. Maple was often used as it gave a cleaner ash. The embers were taken from the oven with an iron ash peel and placed in the small ash oven below. In the very early kitchens there was no ash oven, and the ashes went into the big fireplace or sometimes down a trap door built in front of the hearth. The oven was then swept out with a small birch broom. Next, oak or cabbage leaves were strewn on the floor of the oven, and on these went the loaves. A long, slow baking made bread such as no one knows today.

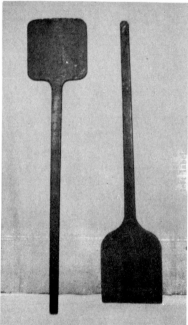

Plate 34. Bread trough with lintel. Paddle for stirring dough and long knife used in cutting dough into loaves; both thirty inches long. Two bread peels, four feet long, used for putting bread into and removing from oven.

The Dutch oven was another place for baking bread. This was the shallow, three-legged kettle with a bail handle and a cover with a rim. Placed in the embers and covered over with them it baked in the same slow way as the brick oven.

Baking in embers was the earliest and only way known to primitive people. The Dutch oven was one of the first kettles and appeared before the brick ovens were added to the open fireplace.

BUTTER MAKING

Cows were imported from England in 1624, a bull and three heifers being the first to come over. The ship *Talbot* landed at Salem, July 20th, 1629, with 12 mares, 30 cows and some goats. Hogs and sheep must have followed in due season for one reads of bacon, pork and sausages and of lamb, veal and mutton, eaten as food. Early records, however, make little mention of the purpose for which cows served except as beef and milk. Hides were used for clothing such as jackets, caps and leggings and also for coverings to trunks. Later accounts tell that the hoofs were used for neatsfoot, which was the binder for paint, and the hairs of the tail went into sieves. It was not until the eighteenth century that the dairy products, butter and cheese, began to appear as food. From then on, until factories took up dairying in 1860, the making of butter and cheese was a never-ceasing labor, the duty of every housewife.

Old agricultural magazines have recorded the first knowledge of butter. Invention ascribes it to the barbarous nations, the ancient Scythians, Germans and Britons. From them the Greeks and Romans learned the art and made use of it at about the time of the Christian era. But it was used only as an ointment and in medicine, and agricultural writers took no notice of it. Ancient butter appears to have been in liquid form, being poured out like oil, and was sometimes burned at the altar and in lamps. Butter of the Bible means thick sour milk or cream. Where olive oil was made, there is little mention of butter.

The American Colonies resorted to wooden buckets for

milking, and the one-handled piggin was used for the last of the milk, called the strippings. The milk was poured into keelers, which were very shallow staved tubs, and set for cream in the cellar or milk room. Skimming the cream off the milk was a daily task, and the collection boasts of the gift of a beautiful shell-shaped skimmer which performed this duty for many a year. Two skimmers were used, one in either hand.

Plate 35. At top, a keeler and a sour cream tub. Below, a butter worker, and a butter scoop for taking butter out of churn.

Plate 36. Butter paddles for working water out of butter. One has a print in handle. The two paddles at right center are machine-made.

Cream was kept in a tub until a necessary amount was ready for making butter. This was called a sour-cream tub. The example pictured stands eighteen inches high, is bound with iron hoops, has a bail handle and a set-in cover, and the old yellow paint still shows. This tub stood in a second-hand shop for a year. The owner became discouraged because the tub took up so much room. He pointed it out to me one day and told me how it had been used for sour cream by an elderly lady in her prime of butter-making. It took very little money to purchase it. It had not been in my collection a week when the cream skimmer was given to me, and these two pieces, the tub and the skimmer, added much to my knowledge of the history of butter-making and gave me further impetus to collecting.

Many butter churns have survived hard usage, although some lack the plunger. They range in size from the small one of fifteen inches to that of twenty-four inches, tapering toward the top and having a set-in cover. The rocking and revolving churn followed the early staved ones and simplified the work.

The grandmothers of long ago tell of using their hands, washed in cold water, for taking the butter out of the churn, although there were scoops for that purpose. The butter was then put into a wooden tray and worked with paddles, called butter workers, until it was free from water. These old butter workers are very common, both those made by hand and the machine-made ones, and they are very often mistaken for scoops. They were used in the hand to press down rather than to scoop, so that the handles are at a different angle than those of regular scoops.

A later butter worker was a frame, wide at one end and narrow at the other, like a fan. The two sides and the narrow end were built up with boards, three or four inches high. A corrugated or plain roller with a handle was set into a slot in the narrow end. The roller was pushed back and forth, smoothing out the butter and pressing out the water. The frame was built on a slant so that the water ran out the slot hole. The roller could be taken out and washed and the frame kept sweet and clean. This invention was placed on a table and by its use more butter could be worked at one time than in the wooden bowls.

Butter made after cattle had been "put out to grass" was universally white. This was remedied by using coloring matter which came from the juice of carrots. The carrots were grated on the tin graters and then simmered in water. The juice was strained and mixed with the cream previous to churning. The custom of coloring poor butter soon became so common a practice that it was ultimately forbidden by law. Food deception began many years ago!

Whatever butter was not needed for home use was packed for market, for selling or for bartering. Large quantities were packed into tubs with a tamp, a flat-headed masher, and leveled off with wooden knives. Butter was also cut and wrapped in pound packages and sold in small quantities. There were butter scales on which to weigh the pound

Plate 37. A pair and a half of palette paddles (see page 84). At right, "Scotch hands" — two paddles machine-made, one hand-made.

blocks. The scales were constructed with two square wooden plates, ten inches square, suspended by cords from a wooden arm. These packages were carried to market in butter boxes. A market butter box with a cover and bail handle was made in factories in the early part of the nineteenth century and listed in catalogues advertising wooden ware.

There were butter testers, both of wood and of iron, for testing butter packed in quantities; long, thin borers, fifteen to eighteen inches in length, with a handle. These were forced into the butter and a section the entire depth of the tub drawn out.

BUTTER MOLDS AND BUTTER PRINTS

Butter molds and butter prints came at a later period when more thought was given to the artistic appearance of food. These are very common and show a great variety of designs. Most of them were produced in factories which continued to sell their products until the last part of the nineteenth century.

The molds are of two styles, cup-shaped and boxed. The cup-shaped ones are both square and round, having the print section separate from the cup. They measure from one inch to four inches in size at the bottom. The butter was packed

[95]

into the moistened holder and then pushed out, shaped and stamped. The box molds were oblong or square in shape, containing several patterns or initials, which printed the butter in sections that could be cut apart. A common factory-period mold is the eight-inch cylindrical one with the inside cut with six sides and which has a stamped, removable bottom. Butter was packed into these box and cylindrical molds with a tamp. An unusual mold is made in the shape of a Maltese cross; this has five sections, four of which are hinged to the fifth, the center. These were held in place with a band while the butter was being packed in. When the mold was opened the butter stood in a square with five sides stamped, each with a different design.

Plate 38. A group of butter prints and molds. The two flat prints and the inverted flat print were also used in cutting cookies. At right, a rare Maltese cross mold.

The butter prints vary in size and the patterns are innumerable. The common shape is round with a protruding handle, a factory-made product. From Pennsylvania came one made with a semi-circular block and another, oblong with two stamped sections.

The prints were shaped on a lathe before they were stamped. Next they were steamed. A design of metal was then laid on the part to be stamped and the pattern forced into the wood under a pressure of one thousand pounds. Another way was to stamp or sketch the pattern on the wood with a pencil, fasten the print on to the lathe and follow the pattern with a chisel. Many prints appear to have been made by this hand-cut and less accurate method.

Although the prints showed many patterns there were but few duplicates. Each family had its own butter design, even as it had its own private cattle-branding design. If their butter pattern was an acorn, all the butter of that family would bear the acorn stamp and would be identified by that design. So there were many patterns for many families. In another section, quite removed, there might appear another acorn, but that would matter little, as the design would not be identical and could in no way hurt the local trade.

"Scotch hands" was the name given to the corrugated paddles which were used for rolling pieces of butter into balls (Plate 37). These were very popular about fifty years ago and were products of factories.

A small tub (Plate 116) in the collection is said to have been used to carry butter into the fields, when the men went to work, or on happy occasions of picnics. It still shows the stain of butter and the odor has not left it.

For such an important industry as butter-making it is little wonder that there had to be a milk room where the butter and the cheeses were made. In later years this room was called the dairy. In one home there was a separate cheese room, with several presses, because of the great amount of cheeses sold.

CHEESE MAKING

Butter was not made during the hot summer months of July and August. The family supply of this commodity was large enough to carry over until fall. During those months the cheeses were made, and the task was a hard one, requiring daily attention.

Plate 39. Cheese drainers. The one shown at upper left, the most primitive type, is in the Farm Museum in Old Hadley, Mass.

From my elderly friend is the following detailed description for making cheese as she made it:

The first step was to prepare the rennet, or runnet. The stomach of a young calf which had never taken anything but milk was used. It was washed, turned and washed again and put into a strong brine. When well salted it was taken out and stretched over a stick to dry. It was then cut into small pieces and placed in jars or a bag called a "cheeselep." Before using, however, it was soaked all day in warm water. The liquid obtained was poured into the milk or cream, standing in tubs, and then stirred with wooden paddles. Coagulation took place and the curds which hardened had to be cut several times. The following morning the curds were put into the cheese drainer.

CHEESE DRAINERS

There is a great variety of cheese drainers. The earliest types were frames of wood, tapering toward the bottom in which was the drain. Sometimes this was a board perforated with holes made by a gimlet; and again rods were fastened across to form a drain. The Windsor type is made of slats or round sticks, such as the name implies. Both styles are pictured. One is square with slats shaped like arrows, having a flat support at the top, and the other is round and made entirely of rounded sticks. They show fine hand work.

The drainer was placed on a rack or tongs, also called a cheese ladder, which rested on a tub. Some early drainers show this ladder made in one piece with the bottom. Cheese-cloth was laid in the drainer and the mixture poured in, filling the drainer. The whey drained through and was given to the pigs; the curds were tied in the cloth and hung up to drain thoroughly. This mass again had to be cut with a curd knife made of wood, or run through a curd breaker, which

[99]

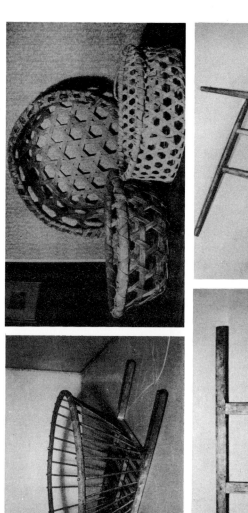

Plate 40. Three cheese ladders or tongs, the one at upper left being a combination drainer and ladder. A trio of cheese baskets is also shown.

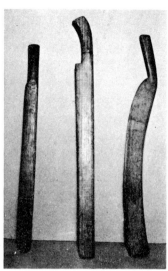

Plate 41. A curd breaker, and three large wooden knives, the first a curd knife, the next a flax breaker and the third a curd knife used also for leveling off butter when packed in a box.

was a box-shaped grinder with wooden teeth. This broken mass was then put into a wooden bowl, salted and worked, and thus made ready for the cheese press.

CHEESE PRESSES

It would seem as if every man had his own kind of press, there are so many creations. The purpose of them was to press and drain the curds of all the whey. The press consisted of two uprights placed on a floor which was called the cheese board. This cheese board had a circular groove in it with a snout in the front. Above this floor, there were two heavy cross pieces which held a large wooden screw, turned by a handle placed horizontally. The screw forced down the lower of the two cross pieces. On the grooved board rested a hoop and this had a round cover which fitted inside. The hoop was lined with cheesecloth, the curds, salted and worked, poured in, the cover called a "foller" placed over it, and the screw turned, pushing down the cover and forcing out the whey. A tub stood under the snout to catch the whey. Often the press was rigged up with pulleys which raised and lowered the cross piece. There were presses which held three cheeses in a row, facilitating the work.

The following morning the cheese was taken out to be dressed. The cheesecloth was taken off and the cheese pared with a wooden knife and made smooth. It was then buttered and a band of cloth, an inch wider than the cheese, was wrapped around it, lapping over fully four inches. This left the top and bottom exposed so that as the cheese was being cured it could be turned and buttered every day. This last process took two weeks, the cheeses having been put into the cheese closet. This closet, described on page 66, was made with four or five shelves and a door frame over which was tacked cheesecloth to let in the air and keep out the cheese fly.

Dutch cheese was made by crumbling cottage cheese and working in butter, salt and chopped sage. Formed into pats, it was set to ripen. Cottage cheese was eaten with molasses on bread like the Yankee combination of pork and molasses.

Cheese was often made with juices which gave it different flavors, adding also to its appearance. Sage cheese was a common variety and this was made by adding the juice of sage leaves or the leaves themselves, chopped finely. Other flavors were made of various herbs and herb teas, and from teas made by boiling young green corn husks or spinach, which gave a fine green color. Pigweed water was used to color the cheese green without giving it any taste.

Three cheeses of fame are recorded in history. In 1802, in the small town of Cheshire, Massachusetts, in the Berk-shires, the women made a cheese weighing 1,450 pounds and sent it to President Jefferson at the White House. "He was

Plate 42. Cheese press, showing hoop, circular drain and snout.

so delighted with it he sent large pungent slices to the governors of the several states."

In the year 1837 a famous cheese was sent to General Jackson in the White House. This cheese was made in Berkshire County, Massachusetts. The town was not recorded but it was presumably Cheshire, as that town boasted of a very flourishing cheese industry. This cheese for General Jackson had a circumference the size of a large carriage wheel and a thickness of the depth of a washtub. In the White House it occupied a spacious room and was attended by ten colored men who were constantly engaged in cutting it into pieces and serving it to the crowds. As an aftermath, the atmosphere of the White House, in spite of "soap, sand and eau de cologne," was almost intolerable for a month.

In 1841 a cheese was sent to President Harrison at the time of his inauguration on March fourth. An account of this was given in the *Evening Mercantile Journal* of Boston on the following June 29th. William Parker of Beavertown, Pennsylvania, took the milk of 32 cows to make this cheese which weighed 194 pounds.

THE SAP INDUSTRY

Sugar maples were very common in New Hampshire, Vermont and New York, and the harvesting of the sugar, which began in February or March, was an annual task. The grove of maple trees was generally a few miles away from the homestead and in it was a cabin and the sugar house. The entire family, including a few extra hands, often went to live in the cabin while the sugaring went on. The perfect weather for sugaring was frosty nights, a westerly wind, and clear thawing days.

The first spiles or spouts were made of sumach or elder

with the pith burned out; later ones were of metal. The sap bucket had one protruding stave in which there was a hole so that the bucket might hang on the spile. Children kept watch of the running sap and when the buckets were full, the sap was poured into the carrying buckets or sap carriers. These had two protruding staves, each with a hole through which a stick was run to serve as a handle. A shoulder yoke was used in carrying these buckets. If the snow was deep and the sugar house far away, the buckets were taken to the sugar house on scoots drawn by oxen.

Fires were kept burning under the huge kettles day and night for three days, and shifts took turn tending them. Little stirring was needed but the sap was closely watched, and the fire was not allowed to go out. Quite often the kettles were swung out in the open on a pole resting in crotches of a tree, many kettles in operation at one time, 4 or even 5. There is a scoop in the collection with a handle more than three feet long and a head seven inches long which was used in stirring the sugar. It is one of the longest scoops made.

The syrup was skimmed, strained through woolen cloths, boiled again and strained again. This process was repeated several times, making the syrup as clear as possible.

The first run of the sap made the purest and the whitest sugar. This was made into cake form for selling. The syrup was poured into a box, sectioned off into pound blocks, or into individual molds similar to those for butter, with elaborate patterns. When the sugar hardened the partitions were pulled out, leaving the separated cakes. The pound blocks were kept for family use and were packed in a large tub and taken to the attic or shed chamber.

The second run of sap was darker and used only for soft sugar. After being boiled down and strained this was poured into covered tubs near the bottom of which was a hole with a wooden stopper or plug. As the sugar hardened, a sugar molasses, called maple molasses, was drawn off and used as sweetening in cooking. Many families knew nothing of sugar or molasses except that which was obtained from the maple trees. This covered tub of soft sugar was also stored in the attic, and the plug kept tight and clean that no ants might gather. In the dry attic the sugar did not mold.

Hundreds of pounds of sugar were sold annually, and a sugar maple grove not only supplied the table with sugar and molasses but was a means of livelihood for many families. A tree fifty years old yielded an average of five pounds of sugar, and they have been known to yield fourteen pounds. The sap industry still survives.

Tracing back the history of white sugar made from the sugar cane, we find that it was used by the Chinese at a very early period, and brought from Asia to Cyprus and Sicily in about the eighth century. In 1240 the sugar industry was introduced into the Madeira Islands. From these islands it was carried to the American Colonies when, by means of trading vessels, masts were exchanged for necessary commodities. By 1747 a beet sugar was discovered in the South, and by 1801 factories were established for the refining of sugar. To most families, however, white sugar was a luxury until well into the nineteenth century.

THE SAUSAGE GUN

By the number of sausage guns found in sheds and attics it would seem that sausage meat was very popular. The lining of the intestines of a hog was used as a casing for chopped meat. The hog's intestine had three layers, the largest of which was the most transparent and was taken for sausage meat. The gun was a sheet-iron tube with a small snout end. The intestine was slipped over the end

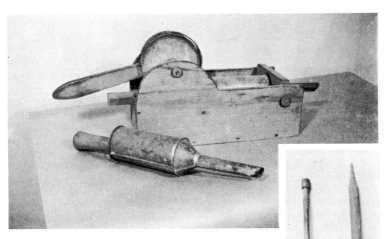

Plate 43. Sausage guns, the smaller one for hand use, the other built with a wheel which operated the plunger. At right, a sausage gun once used in a tavern; measures nearly three feet long.

of the snout of the sausage gun and the meat was forced into the casing with a wooden plunger, shaped like a flat-headed pestle. As the sausage came out the snout, it was tied into sections or links and hung to dry or cure. There were many devices for holding the gun. Up country in a shed chamber, an elaborate invention was found: a box-shaped affair held the tube by means of wooden buttons that locked and unlocked, and a rotating wheel with a handle worked the plunger back and forth. This stood on the table and relieved the worker of holding the weight of the whole gun when making the sausages. Other creations were manipulated by cranks that turned wheels. In a modern age such contrivances would have been patented as labor-saving devices. A new addition to the collection is a sausage gun four feet long with a five-foot plunger, found in a tavern. And the latest is a contrivance of some handy man. The

[107]

gun sets into a hole in a narrow, thin plank, a yard long, on four legs. The plunger is nailed to the middle of a long handle which in turn is fastened to a post at the end of the plank. The plunger was shortened so that it fits into the gun, and the matter of pumping the meat down into the casing was much like the act of pumping water at a pump. The arrangement takes a lot of room, but the job of making the sausages was greatly eased.

THE MAKING OF SOFT SOAP

The wood ashes of maple in the fireplace and bake oven were saved during the winter for fertilizer and for making soap. Soap was made once or twice a year. The ashes were put through a process called leaching to obtain lye for soap. A barrel called a "leach barrel" was filled with a layer of straw, one of lime, one of ashes, and the layers repeated in like manner until the barrel was full. Hickory ashes were considered as fine as maple or birch. Rain water was poured into the barrel every day and seeping through the layers it flowed out a hole at the bottom of the barrel into a tub, as lye. Often the barrel had a perforated bottom. Six bushels of ashes and twenty-four pounds of grease made one barrel of soft soap.

If the barrel had a perforated bottom, it stood on what was called a lye stone — a flat stone having a circular drain cut in it, a little larger round than the barrel. The idea of this was similar to that of the drain in the cheese board floor of the cheese press. The lye stone channel had a run-way out of which the lye ran into a trough connected with a tub at a lower level. Two such stones are being used as doorstones at the Country Store of Wiggins Tavern, North-ampton, Massachusetts. One is a single barrel stone, the other was made for two barrels. It would seem that most of the lye stones have been lost, covered, or are unnoticed. When found, however, they are highly prized.

When the lye was strong enough to float an egg, it was ready to be stirred into the grease that had been saved and clarified for this purpose. If the lye was just right, the soap would "come" quickly, but this was not always the good luck of the housewife. The soap stick was a long wooden stick, made of sassafras wood to give to the greasy mess a pleasing odor. The soap of the old days was known as soft soap and it was kept in barrels and scooped out with a deep, box-like scoop as it was needed. Hard soap was made with tallow from the bayberry.

Plate 44. A dish drainer.

DISH DRAINER

A dish drainer, said to have been made over one hundred years ago, is a very rare piece. The illustration above does not show the exquisite workmanship of fitting and pegging. It is twenty-five inches long, fourteen inches wide and over ten inches deep, with a center bar against which the dishes rested. The wood is much bleached from the lye in the soap and from constant wetting.

The first method of washing clothes was at a near-by brook, with a stone for the washboard and a wooden club for the beater. This custom existed in foreign countries, but it is doubtful if it was carried on among the Colonies for any length of time. For them there was a wash tub in the dooryard, water heated in kettles over fires often built out-of-doors, and wooden washboards on which to rub.

A wash house, a small out-building, was built in some sections, principally in the warmer climes. In this was a brick enclosure for a kettle, with a place for a fire beneath. The kettle was of iron. Wash tubs stood on racks. Among many descendants of the old country, water was boiled with birch ashes and was used as a clothes bleach. This was poured into the tub of clothes, draining out at the bottom through a hole which was plugged or through several holes in the bottom. The operation was repeated three times, the boiling water from the ashes with a strong lye solution bleaching the clothes. The clothes were taken from the water, wrung dry and laid on the grass in the yard or hung on hemp ropes, in sun and wind. A bleaching tub, the bottom of which is filled with holes, stood unnamed until recently, when the process was explained by a young Swedish woman.

The earliest washboard was called a scrubbing stick, and it was just what the name implies. It was a thick, narrow

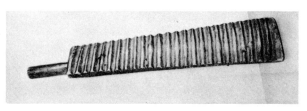

Plate 45. This scrubbing stick may have first been used at the brook.

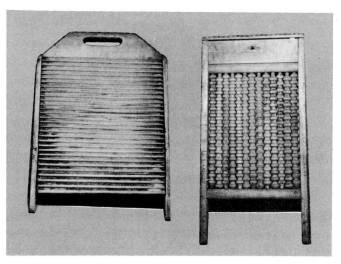

Plate 46. An all-wooden washboard. Reverse side has narrower
corrugations. The other board is of the spool-bed variety.

slab of wood, about two feet long and six inches wide, with
a six-inch handle at one end. One side was flat while the
other side had wide corrugations, cut somewhat pointed.
The scrubbing stick in the collection has corrugations that
were made on a slant, with the idea that the water would
run away from the hand as the clothes were being scrubbed
— provided that you were not left-handed!

A washboard such as is in use at the present time came
next, but it was all of wood. Some have a round hole bored
near the top where the cake of soap lay while the washing
was being done. An unusual one in the collection has corrugations of different sizes on the two sides — wide for the
clothes that were very dirty and narrow for those not so
soiled. The board was in use the day it was purchased.
Another one has wooden spools on which the clothes were
rubbed, this being made in the period of spool beds — some
spools running vertically, others horizontally.

The "dolly" or "dolly pin" must have come next in the

step of progress. This is a heavy wooden club with four deep grooves at the base and a cross-bar handle by which to hold it and turn it about. The idea was taken from the dolly which miners used in separating the ore from the dirt. The dolly is of maple because of the extra weight and the club turned and twisted and mangled the clothes as they lay in the tub with water and homemade soft soap.

The patented washers appeared about the middle of the nineteenth century. They were made with a large corrugated roller with four small rollers placed underneath, revolving as they caught in the grooves of the large roller. This mangled the clothes as they were run through. These washers, in appearance like a wringer, were fastened by metal clamps to tubs, which the buyer had to include in the transaction.

The beginning of the scientific principles of a washing machine was born with the pounder and the pounding barrel.

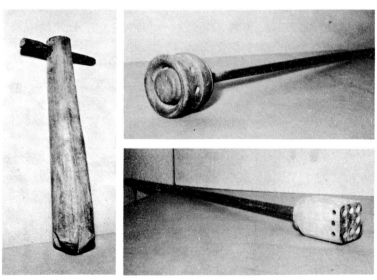

Plate 47. The dolly pin; made to pound and mangle clothes in the wash tub. At right are two pounders, used to pound clothes in a pounding barrel. One is of lignum-vitæ, the other of bird's-eye maple.

[112]

The clothes were put in a barrel and worked up and down with the long-handled pounder. The head of this was a block of wood, shaped and bored with holes to cause suction. Maple was generally used, but a pounder in the collection has a very unusual head of lignum-vitæ. The outer part is cup-shaped with eight holes bored around the edge and the inner part is a flat ball. This principle of suction was the forerunner of washing machines.

WASHING MACHINES

The first washing machines were made in the home work-shop. An oblong or square box was constructed with various inner parts which served to mangle the clothes as they were being washed. Some of these mangle arms were turned by cranks and others played back and forth as the machine was rocked or turned about. The machines were often called cradles, as they stood on legs and were rocked. It would be impossible to describe all of those homemade washing machines. When the factories began to produce them there was established a uniform type, but the progress from those early ones to those manufactured today extended over many generations.

SMOOTHING BOARDS

Before the appearance of flatirons, or sadirons as they were first called (sad meaning heavy), clothes were smoothed with a wooden smoothing board. Remembering that in those early days the washing consisted mainly of bed linen, towels and blankets, one can well see that little ironing was necessary. The smoothing board originated with the people across the water, like many other devices for the home. It is similar to the scrubbing stick with corrugations and has been confused with it. The first thing to look for is the way the corrugations are cut — those of the scrubbing stick are

Plate 48. Smoothing boards, used to roll the sticks on which the sheets were wound. One has a knob for the hand to grasp, while the other has two grooves cut in the edge into which the fingers fitted.

sharp and those of the smoothing board are round. There are two sticks in the collection so nearly alike that it took a bit of shrewdness to tell the difference. The smoothing stick has rounded corrugations and the slab itself was cut in a slight arch. This allowed the hand to be raised from the table as the board was used. At the end, opposite the protruding handle, two notches were cut into which two fingers fitted as the hand gripped the end.

A second and more elaborate smoother has a handle added at one end on the flat side, shaped like a flatiron handle, and at the opposite end a knob, which were used to push the board back and forth as it smoothed the clothes. There are smoothing boards with no corrugations. Handles gave the artistic creators opportunity to design and there are mermaids, lions, bears and other fantastic symbols in live realism. Dates, too, could be added, and they help the research student place the smoothing board as an early conception.

The process of using the smoothing board was explained by a Swedish nurse, who had smoothed with the stick when a child in her native home. The linen to be smoothed was rolled over a wooden roller the size of one's wrist, and about a yard long. (One such roller is being cherished by

Plate 49. A patented washer, an array of clothespins (handmade and lathe-turned), and two clothesline winders.

an elderly lady as one of the last relics of her old home.) The roll was then laid on a table and the smoothing board rolled it back and forth, the board catching it with the corrugations, pressing it and drying it in the same performance. This explains why the smoothing board needed a place for the hand to grip at both ends.

SOAP DISH

A wooden soap dish is a trivial thing, but it adds romance to a collection of wooden ware — a block of wood and a jackknife, and a new one could be had for the asking.

CLOTHESPINS

Clothespins were a sign of progress. The washing in the early days was spread on bushes and on the grass to dry in the sun. When hemp rope appeared, however, clothespins were designed. And designed they were, for out of a collection of twenty-nine, eighteen are different in shape. Birch, maple and hickory were the woods used and the pins were six and eight inches long, sturdily built for the heavy homemade blankets and linen. Clothespins were so easily made at home, both by hand and on the lathe, that it was well toward the end of the nineteenth century before there was an abundance of the machine-made pins. A New Hampshire tin peddler dubbed them "wooden sugar tongs."

CLOTHESLINE FRAMES

Frames on which the clothes lines were wound are occasionally found. One in the collection is made of walnut, with arms fastened with copper nails and with a washer on the handle, giving more play to the arms. Another one is of maple and has a different principle of winding. It would be interesting to know when the custom of stringing the clothesline across the front or side porch came to be in use.

It saved steps, but what of the glorious sunshine out in those open spaces in the yard?

A BRIDE'S DOWRY

In those early days, no bride went to her new home without a large dowry. The family began to lay aside linens as soon as the child was born and it was considered essential that a young woman be amply endowed with these worldly goods. At first thought, it would seem that this custom developed from financial and social reasons. But when one reads deeper into the history of those first years he finds that the large linen dowry was a personal necessity. Washing was done only twice a year, preceding summer and winter, and the need of enough linens to last the season was most essential. Later washing was performed three and finally four times a year. With no conveniences, with the crudest of implements and with heavy homespun linens and blankets, we can well see why the household goods went through the process of being cleaned so infrequently. The weekly wash is a modern arrangement.

SPATULAS, STIRRERS AND MASHERS, MEAT POUNDERS

When old, common-looking wooden sticks found in the discard are examined, they give much valuable information for the research student. The shape, size, workmanship and stains indicate the purpose for which they were originally made.

The long soap stick bleached white, the dye stick stained, the butter paddle showing grease, the hasty pudding stick with its long handle and short head, the round-headed stirrer for pots with bulging sides, the curd breaker shaped like a knife, long and thin, the butter knife also long and thin but stained, the dough paddle and dough knife show-

[117]

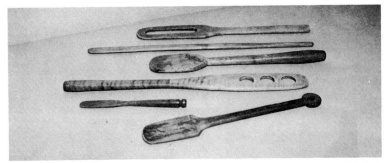

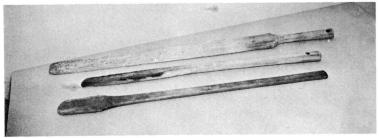

Plate 50. Group of spatulas and stirrers. Below, a hasty pudding
stick, a dye stick and a soap stick.

ing flour whiteness, the short spatula for turning flapjacks,
another spatula for turning apples when drying on the racks,
small stirrers for use in the cooking and beating — these all
make up an interesting array. It would seem as if every
kitchen activity is represented in these implements.

The mashers look very ordinary, but show many patterns.
The one with the large flat head was the butter tamp, used
for pounding the butter into the butter boxes and tubs. The
others were for preparing food.

There were many toddy sticks of all designs. They were
used to crush the lemon and sugar and to stir the drink in
the flip glass or the toddy cup. Sometimes the toddy stick
has a head that is small and flat, and again one that is large
and ball-shaped; and there is one with a corrugated round
head, and another with two heads, one at either end, a small

[118]

one and a large one. There is a toddy spoon with a flat, beveled-edge bowl. Toddy sticks are often confused with wheel drivers used in turning the spinning wheel. In fact, when the wheel driver went astray, the toddy stick did double duty — in the flip glass and for the wheel. The neck of the head is worn thin if it was used to turn the wheel. Those wheel drivers were called fingers or "speed boys" in some localities.

The meat pounders are wooden mallets with the face of

Plate 51. At top, a collection of mashers. The flat one in the foreground was used for tamping butter into boxes. Below, at left is a group of toddy sticks. The two at the right were often used as wheel drivers for the spinning wheel. At the extreme right is a meat pounder.

the head marked in squares, to make for more friction when pounding the meat before it was cooked. They have been mistaken for a branding tool. In a wooden ware catalogue of 1878 they are listed as steak maulers.

There is yet another spatula which has nothing to do with cooking, but which should be described. It is the feather bed smoother. This is paddle-shaped with a short handle,

Plate 52. A feather bed smoother.

the whole measuring about fifteen inches. The only way of distinguishing it from a working tool is the blunt edge — the paddle does not taper at any part of the edge. The feather bed was tossed and stirred up, and flattening it down again was not so simple a trick. If a housewife had no smoother she resorted to a broom handle. A smoother stood in the collection for a year without being identified. One day a visitor told of smoothing out the feather bed, and it took very little imagination to see the possibilities of the unnamed paddle. With more imagination, the two initials, T. L., carved on one side, proved that it was a present to a young bride — made by the hands of her husband-to-be.

It is a wonder that these commonplace wooden imple-ments have survived the years of machine-made pieces. But one of the characteristics of those thrifty housewives was to save, and save they did.

If there is individuality in any of the wooden ware, it is in the scoops and spoons. There are wet scoops and dry scoops, and it would seem as if different ones were to be had only for the asking. A knife and a piece of wood and a fireplace in front of which to work when the day's chores were over — and these necessary tools for the kitchen were created.

Two very rare dippers are pictured. One from Pennsylvania (Plate 53) was made from the root of a tree and shows the gnarly grain, which has been mistaken for burl. The other one (Plate 6), with an upright handle, was turned on a lathe.

The Shaker apple butter scoop is a beautiful thing, and the soft soap scoop, in all its ugliness, is quite the opposite. The apple butter scoop (Plate 24) was used end down while stirring, with the hand pressed on the flat crossbar of

Plate 53. Dipper made from the gnarly root of a tree.
Found in Pennsylvania.

the handle. This one measures fifteen inches in length, perfect in proportions; others are smaller. The soft soap scoop was merely a block of wood hollowed like a box, with a handle added. Some are of one piece of wood. Something

[121]

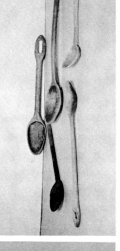
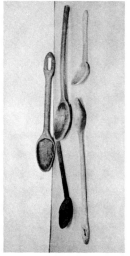
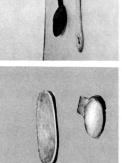

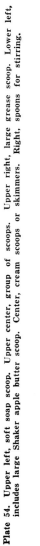

Plate 54. Upper left, soft soap scoop. Upper center, group of scoops. Upper right, large grease scoop. Lower left, includes large Shaker apple butter scoop. Center, cream scoops or skimmers. Right, spoons for stirring.

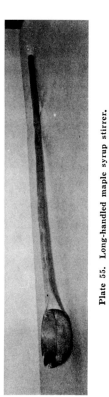

Plate 55. Long-handled maple syrup stirrer.

of this shape was the only means of taking the soft soap from the barrel.

Two-way scoops were inventions of some artistic soul (Plate 24). They had a scoop at one end and a stirrer at the other, and might not have been practical if used in anything but thick apple butter. The mess was stirred with the spatula end and taken out with the spoon part. Probably there were other foods which were stirred by this handy style of scoop.

There is endless variety in the scoops for flour, meal and sugar. They are long and short, narrow and wide, with fancy handles and plain ones. There was no pattern for them until factories began to make them. Some even have the owner's initials cut in them.

A handleless scoop for flour, a delicate shell-shaped scoop for skimming the cream from the milk, a yard-long scoop that stirred the maple syrup, and two that scooped out penny candy in the country store (a penny's worth and a nickel's worth) — this is a collection that leaves nothing to be desired.

The Indian eating scoop (Plate 6) adds much to the collection of scoops. It is doubtful if there is another in existence. It came from Martha's Vineyard where it had been made and used by one of the Indians.

A tool that seems to have no name is a bowl scraper or pusher with which the butter was taken out of the tray. It is a curved piece of wood which fitted the shape of the bowl, with a handle set in at right angles. Held in the hand after it had been pushed through the tray full of butter, the butter was taken from it with a wooden knife and packed into prints.

Spoons were used for stirring and eating. There are not many of them because they were of so little account that

Plate 56. Bowl with scraper used for removing butter from bowl, and
three skimmers, one with perforated lip used for tallow.

they were thrown away. Factory-made spoons replaced the
old ones, and today these are often collected as old because
of their appearance of use and abuse. The new ones can
readily be told by machine-made cutting.

A wooden strainer, a tallow strainer with a cup-shaped
head of tin, and a strainer with a flat tin head, pierced with
holes, make up the family of strainers. An old chopping
tray with a sheet of pierced tin nailed on to the worn-out
bottom served both as a strainer and a grater. Another such
strainer-grater was made like a small picture frame with a
pierced sheet of tin set in.

OTHER PANTRY EQUIPMENT

The display of chopping knives is fascinating. From the
one the handle of which was made from a hickory sapling

[124]

with a narrow band of steel welded on to the U-shaped iron blade which was once a foot-scraper, to the one made of a beautiful piece of steel, shaped and hammered, the array shows every style and size. One has a handle made from

Plate 57. Chopping knives of all types.

[125]

the bone of a lamb's leg, shaped by Nature to fit the hand. The blade of one is ten inches across, corresponding to the width of the long, narrow trays in which fat was chopped. A strange one was made from a cow's yoke fastener with a blade of steel inserted in the end. One was made by cutting out the center part of the head of an ax, making two points which were driven into a handle. Still another was made from part of a scythe. Flat handles, whittled handles, shaped handles. Initials, too, were on some. These chopping knives were never idle, as much food was preserved besides that prepared for the daily meals.

The graters were made by fastening a hammered sheet of tin on to a flat club-shaped handle. The tin was first pierced with a nail, sometimes with the intent of a special design but more often merely as holes. Handmade nails were used in fastening the tin to the wood, showing a pre-factory invention. One grater has initials and a date cut on the

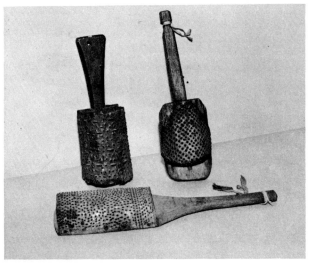

Plate 58. Graters made of pierced tin.

back of it — A. F. Feb 1 1794. These graters were made in the period of Paul Revere lanterns, and one has been previously described made from just such a lantern (Plate 9).

Besides for use in cooking, graters were used to grate carrots for coloring butter. And most important of all was the use of a grater for grating potatoes for starch and for yeast. A grater of enormous size has appeared in the collection, the back board 8 inches wide and 18 inches long. Doubtless with such a grater, the work of grating was more rapid when two hands could work at the same time.

The first lemon squeezer consisted of a handle with a spiral, corrugated head. Digging into the lemon, it forced out the juice, but one would not be sure where that juice went. A later squeezer was made of two arms hinged, one with a rounded projection on which the lemon rested and one with a hollow into which the lemon fitted as it was squeezed. The juice ran out through holes bored in the hollowed section. Someone put his squeezer on a three-legged standard, high enough for a tumbler to stand under it to catch the juice. A long squeezer, about twenty-five inches, was used at clam bakes and rested on a tub. The juice ran out of holes bored in the side of the cup which held the lemon. Lemon juice was prescribed extensively as good for the nerves and as productive of a cheerful disposition.

Patented sifters appeared in the middle of the nineteenth century. Sugar or flour was rubbed through the wire sieve by an arm turned by a crank. These have a patented date stamped on the standard and were the forerunners of metal sifters which are used now.

Every family that kept hogs, and most of them did, made lard. The fat used for lard was found next to the kidneys of the hog and was shaped like a leaf. This gave the

Plate 59. Lemon squeezers. Those at top with corrugated heads; later types in two sections. Large one at left was used at clambakes and rested on the tub in which the lemonade was made. The one at right built on legs to allow for tumbler beneath.

commercial name of leaf lard, meaning that the product was the best. The fat was cooked, tied up in a cloth and squeezed between wooden pinchers called lard squeezers. The liquid was poured into wooden bowls to cool as lard. The part remaining in the cloth was what was known as pork scraps and was considered an addition to any table

[128]

and seen in shops as late as the 19th century. These wooden lard squeezers were easily made — two whittled sticks, flat on one side and rounded on the other, tapered for a handle at one end and curved at the opposite end to allow for motion. These were fastened together with a large wooden peg caught in with a nail, which was left loose to allow for play. Factory-made squeezers were two slabs of wood fastened at one end with a leather hinge, machine-made screws in the leather. A similar two-armed slab was used in cracking lobsters. This was wider than those for making lard, because of the size of lobsters, often five feet long in those first years.

The curd breaker (Plate 41) was another invention which eased the labor of making cheese. When the curds were taken from the drainers they were hard and dry, and before they could be worked into cheese they had to be broken apart and mashed. This was done generally with the long wooden curd knife. But the man who thought of labor-

Plate 60. Patented flour sifter and sugar sifter with label. Cane sugar came to the home in the shape of a cone, weighing from 3 to 30 pounds. Sugar cutters of iron cut off pieces and when the sugar was powdered, it was crushed in a mortar and then sifted.

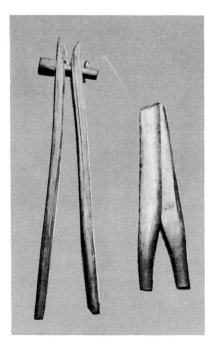

Plate 61. Lard squeezers.

saving devices made a simple device consisting of a box, in which was a wooden roller with long wooden teeth turned by a two-armed crank. This rested over a large bowl or a tub which caught the broken mass as it came through. Some of these curd breakers were made so that the side pieces could be taken out and the roller removed to be washed.

A spice grinder was smaller than a mortar. It was made of two parts, one being cup-shaped with thin points of steel driven into the bottom and the other fitting this cup, with similar points of steel. By turning the two pieces in the hand the spice was crushed and powdered. Another old grinder has a small piece of indented tin on each part.

Funnels were first made of wood. The small ones for the kitchen were factory-made and are about seventy-five years old. They were made on the lathe and are seen in old catalogues illustrating wooden ware. A large funnel made of splint was used for putting vinegar into kegs. Then there were various sizes of tub funnels, made of staves, iron hoops and a short wooden tube in the bottom acting as the funnel. The large one pictured is painted blue and saw hard service in a Vermont sugar grove (Plate 99). Similar ones were used in the process of making cider.

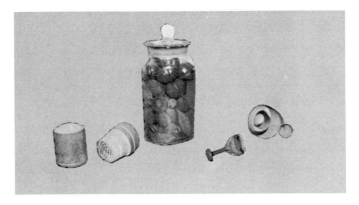

Plate 62. Spice grinder and jar of nutmegs preserved in alcohol more than one hundred years ago. At right is a raisin seeder and doughnut cutter.

The doughnut cutter is a later invention, made of wood instead of the customary tin.

The raisin seeder could not have been very practical in its manner of extracting seeds from raisins. At the end of a wooden handle is a set of wires, inserted in a curve. The tool was rocked back and forth on the raisin and the seeds

Plate 63. Funnels. Small one is of wood, the other of splint (explained in Chapter Eleven on splint).

slipped through the wires, leaving the pulp free and ready for use.

The birch broom did not seem to be considered a pantry tool until it was learned that the small ones were used for beating eggs and whipping cream. Larger ones were used to wash out the maple sugar kettles. These were splintered brooms and are highly prized by families whose ancestors came from across the water where such implements were used. One such broom for beating eggs was brought to one

Plate 64. Splintered birch brooms. Smallest one, six inches long, was used for beating eggs, the other two for sweeping out the bake oven or for cleaning kettles.

of my lectures, but the owner clung to it fondly when persistent offers were made to buy it. Another way of making an egg beater, a bit more sanitary than the splintered broom, was to cut gashes around the end of a small birch twig, up a distance of three inches. Twirling the twig between the palms of the hands beat the eggs in the bowl.

The white man learned from the Indians how to make birch brooms and it came to be called the "Indian broom." It was the yellow birch that was used although in some sections, the blue beech was taken. A sapling was soaked in water, splintered at one end, the core taken out and the splinters tied. Then, back at a distance of the length of the broom head, the stick was splintered, and these strands were turned over to cover the first set of splinters. Three strands were braided and tied around the whole head. The handle was then whittled and smoothed to an even size.

An easier way to make the cleaning broom was merely to splinter the end of the stick and shave the opposite end for the handle. This made a stiffer and thicker broom, one more like a brush. These brooms were used for sweeping

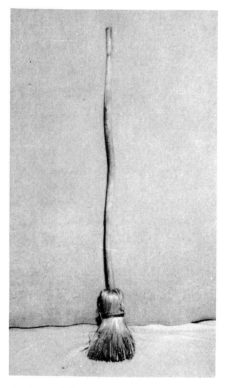

Plate 65. Splintered birch, or Indian broom, four feet or more in length.

out the ovens before the bread was set to bake, as well as
for washing out the kettles.

The broom for sweeping the floor is also pictured. But
another kind of floor broom was more common and easier
to make, consisting of birch twigs fastened to a handle, tied
with birch withes or with coarse rope. This is such a broom
as the witches rode in the sky! Brooms go back as far as
the Roman bakers and millers, who used brooms made of
palm leaves.

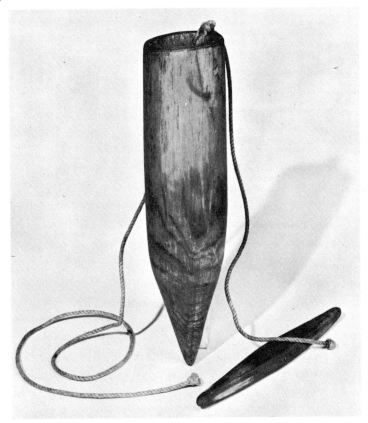

Plate 65a. This wooden container held water for the whetstone. It was tied around
the waist and thrust into the ground upon arrival at the field.

Fig. 1. A one-of-a-kind butter trough in which butter was worked. The snout at the end has a channel out of which the liquid was poured. Two butter workers are shown -- one of burl and the other of curly maple.

Fig. 2. Scales for weighing butter. Some stood on a standard and others hung. This one has pieces of lead attached to two cords to make an even balance.

Fig. 3. Butter prints. A cow at the left and an eagle at the right. A rare shape is the elliptical one.

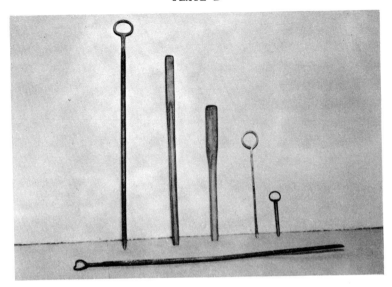

Fig. 1. A set of testers. The extreme left and one in front are iron and the next two are wood. These were butter testers. The short one at right was a cheese tester. Plunging the tool into the butter or cheese drew out a sample. The one second from right is a large steel marrow scoop, used when bones were boiled and served for their marrow.

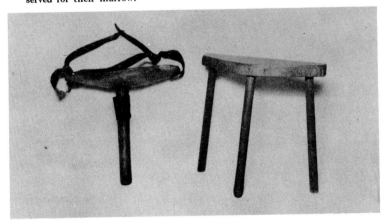

Fig. 2. On the left an unusual one-legged milk stool which strapped to the man could be worn while walking. The shaped seat has 6 carved hex mark circles with elliptical decorations. Note the holder for the rag! The three-legged stool on the right balanced well.

PLATE C

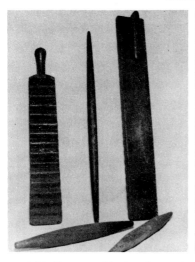

Fig. 1 (L). Two smoothing boards complete with smoothing sticks. The long one was
for sheets folded four times and the short ones for pillow cases or biers. The ends
taper to allow for hems or folds. Fig. 2 (R). The first washer with a suction
cup. The crank worked the plunger up and down. The stick adjusted the
distance from the clothes.

Fig, 3. Two soft soap scoops with handles made from one piece of wood are shown
here with two soap holders. They all show the effects of lye.

Fig. 4. A pounder for clothes -- factory made with a label of directions. Soap was
put into the container and the cover clamped down. Working this up and down
made suds come through the four openings at the bottom. A time saver!

Fig. 1. Apple parer that screwed to a table. The blade is in a
handle tied to the parer to keep it from getting lost.

Fig. 2. A Pennsylvania apple butter stirrer with a nine-foot long handle and a
two-foot long head, filled with holes. The worker stood outside the window away
from the heat of the kettle, dragging the stirrer back and forth in the kettle.

Fig. 3. Apple grinder with metal teeth used to grind apples into pomace.

CHAPTER SIX

Bowls, Plates, Mortars and Pestles — Production of
Hand Labor and of the Early Lathes

At the same time that the Colonists were creating the pantry tools with which they worked, they were fashioning their bowls and plates on which to eat. The handy man of the house took this task upon himself, but if he lacked that particular talent there was always a dish turner in the village who supplied the necessary receptacles.

Man's first utensils were of stone. Grinding and crushing were done with stones and stones served as eating and cooking utensils. The North American Indians and the white man learned to use wood, surrounded as they were with vast forests.

BOWLS MADE FROM THE BURL

There was one particular part of the tree which was found to be the best for bowls. That was the tumor, or the wart. The Indian called it the knot and the white man called it the burl, or the knurl. It is the diseased growth found on the elm, ash, birch, chestnut, walnut and maple trees. The only burls usable were those on the maple and ash trees, the others being too porous, although an occasional bowl made of walnut has been found. The grain of the burl is peculiarly marked with spots, is gnarly and cannot be mistaken as being anything but the burl. The shape of the growth also lent itself to that which was needed for a bowl. Walnut burl was used for inlay in fine furniture.

After the growth was removed from the tree the bark was cleaned off and the wood left to be air-dried. Then a fire was started on the flat side and allowed to burn until

Plate 66. Burls. At left, a maple burl from the collection. Center, one of the seven burls on the huge old elm at Deerfield, Mass. At right, another step in the process of making a bowl. (From the collection of Mr. A. B. Wells of Southbridge, Mass.)

the wood became charred. When the burl was thus soft-
ened, the first cutting was less difficult. The Indians' tools
were of flint, stone and shell, and they hollowed out the
growth most laboriously — time and patience being the chief
requisites.

INDIANS' BOWLS

The Indians' bowls were oval in shape and deep, with
two handle holes, and they show the mark of the tools. One
such bowl is pictured. It is not of burl, however, but of

Plate 67. Upper left, Indian bowl made in 1803 from poplar, not from a burl. At
right, Indian bowl made from an ash burl. (In the collection of Mr. A. B. Wells of
Southbridge, Mass.) Center, rare burl bowl of ash, showing unusual marking.
Lower left, burl bowl showing the stain of grease. Right, burl bowl showing the
whiteness of milk or bread dough.

poplar, cut with the grain of the wood. It was made in
1803 by an Indian named Huge Pie of New York State,
and given to one Charity Hunt, whose granddaughter, an

[137]

elderly lady, sold it. The bowl must have had hard usage, for the handle at one time was broken off and pegged on with wooden pegs, only to be broken off again and lost. The broken pegs still show.

Plate 68. Rare cheese drainer from the collection of the late Mr. Charles L. Hopkins of Francestown, N. H., showing method of fastening on the cheesecloth by means of pegs.

COLONISTS' BOWLS

The burl bowls of the Colonists, with some exceptions of course, were made on the lathe, first on the spring pole lathe and later on the mandrel lathe. A tool belonging to the chisel family was used to hollow out the wood as it seesawed or rotated on the lathe. The end of this iron tool was flattened into a thin strip, which was sharpened and which curled over, making a two-edged blade, nearly a full circle. The work could be done fairly rapidly as compared with the cutting of the Indians' flint. The round bowls often have a beveled edge, and grooves were cut on the outside surface for ornamentation.

The large burl bowl pictured is as beautiful a bowl as ever could be found. Its unusual markings show the rings of the tree itself where the burl began to grow. It was never used as a chopping bowl as there are no cuts in it, and one can well visualize the bowl as holding the noontime dinner. It is an ash burl (Plate 67, center).

A bowl is a bowl to the casual observer, but to the research student the study goes deeper than the surface.

Grease stain in the wood means that the bowl was used to hold grease and fat. The grease penetrated the wood and darkened it and no amount of cleansing can remove it. The bowl is shallow with rounded sides, as shown in illustration.

Quite the opposite appearance is found in the whiteness of the bowl that held milk. The milk bowl or tray was made much like the earthenware bowls, with shallow, straight side and a large bottom.

The butter tray was made in a shape similar to the milk bowl but with more depth. Butter was worked in this bowl after it was taken from the churn, and the one illustrated shows the line of the fat.

The cheese drainer is an unusual bowl. This has a hole in the bottom which is covered with a piece of cheesecloth, which served as a strainer. The cloth is fastened up on the sides of the bowl by loops at the four corners held by wooden pegs near the edge of the bowl. Another cheese drainer has a flared edge around the rim of the hole in the bottom. An elastic was run through the hem of a circular piece of cheese-cloth and this set tight over the rim of the hole. The cloth was taken off and washed after each operation and doubtless had to be renewed quite frequently. The wood bleached by the cheese shows in the picture.

Bread was often made in a bowl instead of a bread trough. This bowl was a deep round one, and here again is seen a whiteness in the wood and a cleanness.

Bowls were used on the table to hold the meat stews, puddings, or other parts of the dinner. From these bowls individual members of the family would fill their smaller bowls, which were of many sizes.

The wash bowl is shaped either like the ordinary earthen-ware bowl or like the tin basin. They would stand hard usage, and were kept on a bench outside the back door ready for the family's ablutions at meal times.

Most bowls met the chopping knife sooner or later and marks of the chopper are plainly visible. Because of this final use of a bowl, the shape and stains should be studied carefully to determine the purpose for which the bowl was originally made.

Eating bowls were often made from the burl. One in the collection is like a shallow soup plate, while another is a small, deep bowl. The eating bowls most commonly found, however, are not of the burl, and the workmanship is of a more recent date. They are roughly turned as if they were factory products and are made mostly of chestnut, although some of the better ones are of maple or pine.

Plate 69. Three eating bowls and at right a wash bowl.

The burl was used for things other than the bowls — for salts, goblets, butter workers, mortars, the round head of large shovels (the long handle taken from the tree trunk),

Plate 70. Mortars made from the burl.

covered dishes and urns. These all withstood hard usage and exposure and are very beautiful and ornamental.

WOODEN BOWLS OTHER THAN BURL

Especially interesting are the large and long chopping bowls made from the trunk of the tree, cut with the grain. Some are the length of the reach of the arm and the width of a long chopping knife. These could be held on the knees. Others are large and heavy and stood on the table while the chopping was being done. Great quantities of fat and meat went under the chopper for the food to be preserved for

[141]

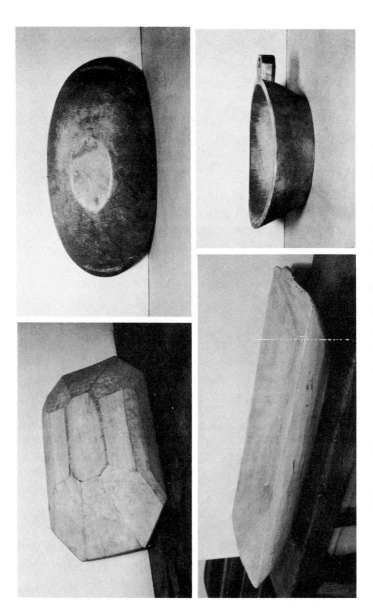

Plate 71. Three interesting chopping bowls and a wash bowl. Upper left, octagon chopping bowl, unusual in cutting. At right, an oval machine-made bowl with notched handles.

the long winter months. Families were large, and the chopping tray was seldom idle.

The most common bowls are round. They were turned on the lathe more easily than the work could be done by hand. Chestnut, maple and pine are woods used in these bowls.

The oblong, hand-hewn bowl is very often seen. Such are of maple, made from wood taken from the heart of the tree, as the round ones were, and they show the marks of the hand tools, the knife and adze. The sides are cut down straight to a flat bottom, and sometimes cut-in grooves were made for handles. An unusually elaborate one is pictured, octagon in shape, each surface accurately cut and smoothed.

The oval bowls with the lips at either end for handles appear to be factory-made. They are lathe-turned and are found in many sizes and have no particular interest for the collector.

There are two rare bowls in the collection which have a colorful history. One (Plate 18) is a large, round bowl to which copper handles were fastened. It came from the Shaker Colony, formerly in Enfield, New Hampshire, but abandoned some years ago. A carpenter from Worcester, Massachusetts, working on the job of dismantling the place, brought home several unusual pieces which appealed to him, and this bowl was one of them. The eating bowl has gray-green paint on it and two large copper handles were screwed on to the edge.

A second rare find was the bowl of lignum-vitæ. In the Marine Hospital on Martha's Vineyard lives an elderly retired seaman who, with his wife, conducted an antique shop. The day I visited him in his shop I had my picture album with me to better explain what my wooden ware included. Excusing himself, he went out and when he returned he was carrying a beautiful chopping bowl made in the shape of a soup tureen. I made an offer at once, but the little old sea captain would not consider it. I browsed around the shop for a long time, listening to old tales of this and that and learning valuable history. When ready to go I again made an offer for the bowl, increasing the amount of my first sum and, to my joy, the transaction was made. But as he took the bowl out to the automobile, he could not keep back the tears, telling me again how it had been made on his father's whaling vessel, sailing out of New Bedford. A

Plate 72. a, b, Two bird's-eye maple bowls; c, a deep salt bowl used in feeding cattle; d, shallow fruit-drying bowl; e, bowl of lignum-vitæ, made on a whaling vessel.

feeling of pleasure was mixed with the sadness, for the bowl was going to be in an historical collection.

Lignum-vitæ was such a heavy wood it could well be used for bowls on whaling vessels, breasting stormy seas. These vessels returned with this wood in their cargo and the sailors made utensils in their leisure time. This particular chopping bowl was in the ship's cupboard for many years and the worn center vouches for that fact; the level of the inside of the bowl has been worn down at least two inches.

Another wood besides lignum-vitæ which made beautiful bowls was bird's-eye maple. Two are pictured, and the tiny eyes can be seen.

There is a very odd flat bowl that came from New York State (Plate 72d). It is oval in shape, twenty-eight by nineteen inches, with two small handle lips, and very light in weight, being made of whitewood. Fruit was placed on it to dry in the sunshine.

The salt bowls (Plate 19) are lathe-turned and vary in size from the large one of seven inches to the individual one of two inches. The salt bowl is a round bowl, plain or with grooves, made of pine or maple with an occasional one of burl. There is one bowl that is like a small oval chopping bowl, measuring a foot long and four inches deep, which was used when feeding salt to cattle. There are marks on the inside edge of the bowl showing where the tongues of the animals had licked the wood clean when taking the salt.

TRENCHERS, PLATES AND PLATTERS

The early name for the wooden plate was trencher, and the man who ate from one was called a trencherman. Two people eating from the same trencher were called trencher mates. The word trencher originated in England, meaning "to cut" or "to carve." The English trencher is square and thick and in one corner is a hollowed-out place for salt or condiment. There are often inscriptions or bits of verse around the edge, making a more ornamental plate than those of early America. The plates made in this country were round. The custom of using the reverse side for a second course originated in England and must have clung to the generations here, for marks are seen which would strengthen the story. We hear it said that there was a dinner side and a pie side. Trenchers were advertised as late as 1775 in the *Connecticut Courant*.

The square trencher was made by hand, and the lathe was used to make the hollow center and the indentation for the salt. The round trencher was turned on the lathe

Plate 73. A collection of wooden plates.

and the man who did this work was called a dish turner. The wood used was maple, birch, beech or ash. The four-teen-inch plate in the collection is said to have come from England and is made of English ash.

[146]

Plate 74. At left, a rare mortar of lignum-vitæ. The center mortar stands twenty-eight inches high and was used for pounding corn for samp; the pestle was a shaped stone. The mortar at right is twenty-one inches high with a pestle forty-two inches long, and was used for pounding barley.

There are many wooden plates being manufactured now, and the collector must be skillful in detecting the old from the new. Varnish covers the wood, but a connoisseur will detect the feel and lightness of any old wood against the new wood. Much wooden ware is being made and has its rightful place but none of it should be added to collections.

Platters were apparently used more commonly in New York State and Pennsylvania than in the New England Colonies. The bowl was more to the housewife's liking generally. Platters were mentioned in lists of things brought over from England. They were both oval and oblong and were made of ash, maple and pine. The collection boasts of a wooden platter, one for serving a roast pig, thirty-five inches long, a rim six inches deep on the inside, the bottom one inch thick, the whole cut from one piece of pine wood. It was used in a tavern and doubtless many a pig was served, roasted to a turn, with a red apple in its jaws.

Bread boards appeared at a later time, on which bread was cut at the table. These are round and, more often than not, have an ornamental edge of flowers and fruit, stamped by machinery in the same manner as the patterns on the butter prints. "The Staff of Life" explains the use of the board. A butter dish with the word "Butter" in the design kept company with the bread boards fifty-odd years ago.

MORTARS AND PESTLES

The first grinding and crushing were done with stones. A stone hollowed by Nature was the receptacle and another stone was used as a crusher, either long like a roller or chubby like a club. Following this age came the period of wood, and mortars and pestles for the barn and for the home were made from the trees. The Indians conceived the idea of fastening the pestle to a slender sapling and pulling it down to the mortar, both mortar and pestle being stone. When released, the sapling lifted the pestle, thus taking the weight from the worker. This arrangement was used by the

Plate 75. A group of mortars. One at extreme left is of lignum-vitæ; the next a spice mortar of maple. At extreme right is a snuff mortar, and the small one in the foreground was used in a doctor's office. The large pestle is a gnarled root.

[148]

white man and he made further service of it, that of signaling to a distant neighbor. The echo of the blows carried in the wind, and the messages, sent both in a friendly manner and in times of distress, could be ciphered by those listening.

Large mortars, standing two and three feet high, were used in the barn for pounding and crushing grain before the time of mills. A rare one in the collection, illustrated, stands twenty-one inches high with a chopping depth of sixteen inches and an opening of fourteen inches. The base of a red ash or a swamp ash was used, and the lines of a drawknife show that it was made by hand. It is shaped like an egg cup with a base standard, and it still shows the worn green paint. The pestle is a hickory sapling, standing forty-two inches high and cut with pounding knobs at either end. This mortar and pestle was used to crush barley for the oil, and having been in use for many years the pestle has worn a deep pocket in the bottom of the mortar.

CORN MORTARS

Another large mortar was used for pounding kernels of corn, first soaked in water, into coarse powder known as samp. This meal was used for porridge, which the Indians showed the white man how to make. The mortar stands twenty-eight inches high, but has an inside cavity only six inches deep and nine inches across, the size of a pumpkin. The pestle for this was a shaped stone, about a foot long, as the corn called for considerable weight to crush it. Another pestle used in the shallow mortars was made from the right-angle joint of a limb and tree. This took more muscle, as the worker had to make up for the lack of weight in the stone pestle. All of these large mortars for use in the barn

[149]

were made from the base of a tree, and it mattered little how large they were or in what shape they were cut.

FAMILY MORTARS

The mortars for family use were many and varied. Everything came to the home in coarse form and had to be ground and crushed before being used — salt, sugar, herbs, soda and spices. The common mortar was of maple or pine, turned on the lathe in uniform shape, six to ten inches high, with deep cavities. The pestle was a shaped pounder of no particular interest, with few exceptions.

Lignum-vitæ mortars are very ornamental when they show the two shades of the wood, the sap wood and the heart. The pestles of these are of lignum-vitæ, too, but the pestles often became separated from their mortars and stray pestles do not match the mortars.

Different again are the mortars of burl. Burl was not used for pestles for some unknown reason, so maple pestles were the rule. One burl mortar has a pestle of oak with a tip of iron ending in a ball. The weight of the head has worn the mortar nearly through.

Another unusual wood for a mortar is curly maple. This has been incorrectly called a burl because the wood is so mottled. The pestle is maple, cut with a long slender handle with a ball head. A curly birch mortar with a curly birch pestle lends itself to the picturesque array.

Whitest and daintiest of all is the birch spice mortar. It was made urn shape, hollowed to a thinness, with a deep cavity, and the pestle has a small snub end. It never saw hard use, having been made only for spices.

Another uncommon mortar was the one for powdering snuff. This one was made from chestnut with a cavity scarcely two inches deep, as snuff was powdered in small

Plate 76. At left, birch mortar with curly birch pestle. Center, bird's-eye maple mortar. At right, covered mortar.

quantities. The pestle is also of chestnut with a snubby end.

There was both a quassia cup and a quassia mortar. A cup was made from the wood and this filled with water produced a drink containing medicinal properties. A small mortar was made from the wood and used in crushing the bark or chips of the wood of the tree to be used in medicine. The mortar stands only five inches high with a two-inch pestle. A negro named Quassi accidently discovered the medicinal properties of the tree, supposedly in 1756 (another date is 1730), thus giving the name Quassia to the tree.

Plate 77. Quassia cups and quassia mortar. Made from a tree containing medicinal properties discovered by a negro by the name of Quassi. Water from these cups was supposed to contain medicinal values.

Small mortars were used in doctors' offices for powdering herbs for medicine. One in the collection stands three inches high with a pestle four inches long. Mortars of brass and iron were first brought to this country and later made here, while others were made of stone, soapstone and wedge-wood. These were used particularly in medicinal work as wood was not considered as suitable as other materials. The early homes knew naught of wood for kitchen or fireside utensils, using those of brass and iron, brought from across the water.

Pestles were often a gnarled piece of root, shaped ready for use. These roots were extremely hard and likely to with-stand years of continuous use. Iron-headed pestles, while not common, were very effective because of the extra weight.

Mashers are odd pestles for the pantry, used in preparing food. All the equipment required for making these was a piece of wood and a jacknife — any handy man could whit-tle and turn one out in spare time.

Mortars, pestles and mashers are still kept about the house and used for the same purposes for which they were made.

Plate 77a. Two burl dippers. The bowl came from the burl
and the handle from the trunk of the tree.

[152]

Fig. 1. Pig platter made from one piece of wood three feet long. A roasted pig was served head, feet and tail with an apple in its mouth.

Fig. 2. Remember when the bread was placed on a bread board and cut at the table? One says Bread, one says Spare Not. Still another says The Staff of Life. The small butter dish says Butter.

Fig. 3. A group of pantry mortars and pestles. The one at extreme right is lignum-vitae showing the heart and sap. The large central one is also of lignum-vitae, the heart wood. The one at the left is burl with an iron headed pestle.

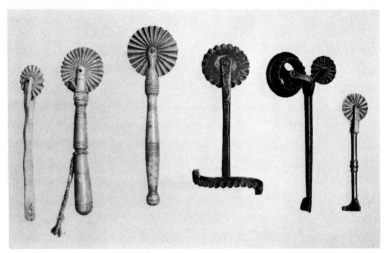

Fig. 1. A rare array of pastry jiggers or crimpers. The three at left are whale bone. The one at extreme right is cast brass and the other two are iron. The second from the right is cast while the one with the long curved end is hand wrought. These were used to run around the edge of the pie and to cut out cookies that had been made with designs.

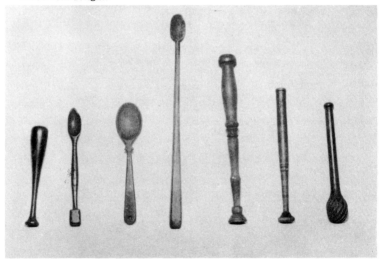

Fig. 2. A row of Toddy Stirrers. The wear on the neck of the one at the right reveals that it was used also as a spinning wheel driver or speed boy.

Fig. 1. A pair of feed bags for horses with solid weaving.

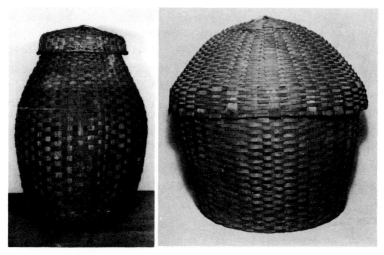

Fig. 2 (L). This splint goose basket, standing over three feet high, was used not only at plucking-time but to hold the feathers afterwards. Fig. 3 (R). A rare feather bed basket of splint, measuring a yard in diameter. It was used in summer when the bed was not needed.

Fig. 1. A sheep yoke to keep the sheep from jumping a wall. A horse hobble with two ankle yokes and a long chain with a swivel.

Fig. 2. Sheep stamps, hand whittled. They count up to seven, probably the number the owner possessed. The stamps show that a red grease was first used, probably made from red clay. The last smear shows a black, tar substance.

CHAPTER SEVEN

Common Wooden Boxes that Graced the Pantry Shelves —
Condiments from Foreign Shores

A PANTRY could never have been a pantry without boxes in which to keep things. Today there is an array of many-colored tins and jars, but grandma's pantry knew only the wooden boxes. They stood there in graded nests or as single receptacles, oval or round, painted and unpainted. And they held the spices, herbs, the "sody" and the meals.

It is interesting to note that in a collection of over two hundred boxes, such as mine, there are few which are alike. Size and workmanship vary, and several kinds of wood are found. There are boxes made by the Shakers and those made by the Colonists.

Before the open fire in the long winter evenings, grandpa loved to whittle. Whenever certain things were needed they were easily supplied with a piece of wood and a jackknife. For the boxes, strips of wood had been obtained from the sawmill for which grandpa had "traded a bargain" with butter, cheese or eggs, and sometimes extra logs were used in the transaction.

MAKING BOXES ON MOLDS

The process of making a box was somewhat difficult. There was a block, called a mold, which was used in shaping the box. There must have been many molds for the various-sized boxes, both round and oval. From the bottom, a protruding arm extended which was held in a vise or placed on the floor between the feet when used. Down the side of the mold was a strip of metal on which the nails were pounded when the rim of the box was fastened together.

There are two sets of molds in the collection, having neither a protruding arm nor a strip of metal. These must have been used in the lap or on a table.

Grandpa cut a strip of wood the width that he wished, cut a point at one end and plunged the strip into a kettle of hot water hanging on the crane over the fire. While this was soaking he took the wooden gauge, which was similar to a compass, and marked out on a piece of pine the cover and the bottom for the box. If it was to be round, one circle was enough, but if it was to be oval, it took a bit of skill to mark it with the compass. Sometimes two circles were enough, but quite often a geometrical figure was inscribed with several

Plate 78. At left, round boxes produced by the Colonists; the nest of oval boxes at right was made by the Shakers.

[154]

arcs, which show on several boxes, to obtain the curved ends of the oval. The moistened strip was then taken from the water and wrapped around the mold. The ends were fastened with spear-pointed nails which flattened into a letter J when pounded on the metal strip. (For the big boxes there were hand-cut nails with rounded heads.) This done, the bottom had to be fitted in and set snugly, and grandpa used wooden shoe pegs for his nails. The cover was made in the same way on a mold which was a trifle larger than the one for the box, so that the cover would fit over the box. Grandpa was free to make any kind of a lap on the box; sometimes he made a short lap, sometimes a long one, sometimes no lap at all but just a seam. It must have been fun to think out different ways to make boxes for the pantry shelf.

The molds for the boxes are seldom found now, probably having been destroyed. A few can be seen in the New York State Museum in Albany, and pictures of them are shown in *The Community Industries of the Shakers*.

The boxes range in size from twenty-four inches in diameter for cheese to one and one-half inches for pills. There are oval ones for herbs, measuring eighteen inches in length, and oval ones for pills only two inches long. The odd boxes with fancy laps were either round or oval, and the nests of round boxes followed later. The round nests appear to be factory made, and we find that factories started putting out this wooden ware in Hingham, Massachusetts, in 1850. The wood of the factory-made box has a different "feel," and the fastenings are either black or copper nails. Inventories, dated as early as 1634, mention nests of boxes and state their value, but it is probable that none of these exist today.

Plate 79. At top, staved and hooped butter boxes. Center, cheese boxes of
early factory period. Those at bottom show hand workmanship.

The first Shaker Society was established in this country in 1787. These consecrated people not only lived a life of rigid rules but made their productions conform to strict and uniform workmanship. The Shaker industries were run on a commercial basis. They not only had large outputs of medicines, herbs, seeds, chairs and brooms but they invented and patented machines to facilitate production. A standard uniformity is found in their nests of oval boxes made at first with twelve in a set, later with nine, seven, and then five. The laps of the box, the points, or "fingers" as they were called, were graded in number from four in the largest size to two in the smallest, and the point in the cover rim turns in the same direction as that of the box. This is noted as a distinct characteristic of the Shaker boxes. The points of one broken set of boxes have a left-handed turn, as if made by a left-handed man.

A second characteristic of the Shaker box is the copper nails used in the laps and for fastening the bottom and top to their rims. There are no wooden pegs as in the Colonists' boxes. The Shaker box is uniformly made of maple, with pine for the tops and bottoms. There is no such variety of woods as was used by the Colonists. Beauty was secondary to utilitarianism, and this restraint is shown in everything pertaining to the Shakers.

There is no way of telling the exact age of wooden boxes. Beyond the fact that they are hand made with handmade nails, we must be content with the scant notice they have been given. They are listed in inventories as early as 1660. Shaker history mentions them in 1798, and a box in the collection, coming from England, has 1764 painted in red.

In classifying the boxes, I have divided them into four groups: the largest size for butter, cheese and herbs; the next for meals and sugar; the next smaller for spices; and the smallest for pills. Having said that the Shaker nests of boxes were uniformly made, the descriptions that follow explain the many and varied shapes of those made by the Colonists.

BUTTER BOXES

The butter boxes were made of pine staves, with oak, ash or hickory hoops, a pine bottom and a pine cover with a rim of the same wood as the hoops. Occasionally the staves were dowelled together, a process of fastening by means of a peg driven into one side of a stave and fitting into a hole in the abutting stave. Each stave had two dowell pins, one at the top and one at the bottom, and besides holding the staves securely they allowed for the expansion and contrac- tion necessary for boxes which held butter. The bottom of the box was a piece of pine, first marked circular with the divider or compass and then cut with the cooper's shave while being held in a vise. Sometimes the bottom was made of two pieces of wood dowelled together to prevent warping. The edge of this circular bottom was beveled with a cham- fering knife or chamfer. This beveled edge set into grooves at the lower edge of the staves. These grooves, called the croze or the furrow, were made with a knife known as the croze, which in turn was held on a croze block. The ends of the staves were smoothed with a knife known as the leveler. The hoops were split with a splitting hook and then shaved on a shaving horse — a plane fastened to a bench on legs on which the worker sat as he planed. A clamp held the hoop as it was being shaved with what was called a hoop shave. It has been claimed that hand-rived shingles, shaved on a shaving horse, shed water, whereas cut staves held the water. This would account for the old unpainted houses remaining in good condition, another reason aside from the shingles having been air-dried.

The hoops on the butter boxes show two types of fastenings, and judged by workmanship the age of the box is told by the manner of the fastening of the hoops. They are called locked laps. The earlier type has the ends fashioned like an arrow point with a notch near the end, and these ends tuck under and lock at the lap and do not slip apart.

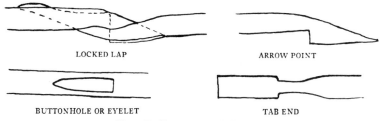

LOCKED LAP   ARROW POINT

BUTTONHOLE OR EYELET   TAB END

Plate 80. Two types of locked laps.

The second type of locked lap is the one made similar to a buttonhole and tab end. One end has a slot cut in it and the other is tapered, and with the hoop made pliable, either by steam or by soaking in water, the tapered end slips into the slot, opens flat again and locks. A peg inserted at the center point of the lock makes it more secure. This is the more common lap of the hoops on the staved butter boxes.

Butter was put into the box with a tamp — a flat-headed masher — and leveled off with a wooden knife. A box that was staved had a chance to expand with the moisture, and the cover with its hooped rim fitted very tight. The lapped box could not have been packed with butter because there was no leeway for the nails in the lap to give, and the sides would pull away from the bottom. A second reason lay in the fact that the nails would affect the butter if they came in contact with it. All the wood of the staved, hooped box was pine — staves, top and bottom. This was the odorless, white pine. On the other hand, the wood of the lapped box was ash, oak and maple, and these woods were not suitable

Plate 81. Box used in carrying butter to market;
also used as a sugar box.

for butter. When in later years butter was cut in pound packages and wrapped, the lapped boxes were used for carrying the butter to market, and those boxes were made as deep as a pound of butter standing on end.

Much confusion has come from the indiscriminate way of calling all the large wooden boxes cheese boxes. The manner in which one generation used these boxes was not necessarily followed by another generation, but the foregoing description of the two types of boxes definitely explains their differences as they were originally planned and made.

CHEESE BOXES

Several cheese boxes shown in the illustration (Plate 79) have individual workmanship. One is the cleanest and freshest box imaginable, made of maple, with pine top and bottom, and fastened with large, convex hammer-headed nails. A second one is crudely made of thick, roughly-cut wood, and it is so heavy it seems as if it contained a cheese. Another one is of a later factory period, having machine-made nails. Still another is oddly made with a long pointed lap on the box and on the cover rim, and this too was fastened with large handmade nails.

The commonly known cheese box is the factory-made box, three of which are pictured. They are uniformly made with copper nails fastening the laps. Quartered oak was often used which made a beautifully grained box — the flecks of the grain show like moiré or watered ribbon.

The box with which the collection was started was a lapped cheese box. It was painted green with the name "S. Reed" (see page 1) stamped in yellow on the bottom, coming from the town of Oakham, Massachusetts, the childhood town of my father. After the box was scraped and stained so that it might be used, the woods were found to be ash, hickory and pine, the nails were copper, while wooden pegs held the top and the bottom to their respective rims.

After this book was well under way a number of new pieces found a place in my collection. One of the rare finds was a pie box, pictured in Plate 92. It is not unlike a cheese box in size, but is deeper. A rack was made, the size of the box, with three small legs, making it possible to carry two pies in the box — a pie under and on the rack. At sociable gatherings, it was a custom then as now to take food, and the pie box made it possible to take pies with no mishap.

THE HERB BOX

The herb box was a large oval box and was made in various sizes, either shallow or deep. Few have survived and so far only five have found their way into the collection, two of the Shaker production and three from the Colonists. The choicest box in the collection is the large red herb box with an irregularly-cut lap extending along the entire side and nailed with copper nails. The box is seventeen and

Plate 82. Large herb box painted a coffin red, shown with pill boxes and a box lined with calico and used for jewelry.

Plate 83. a, Shaker herb box showing water line where it floated for many days at Storrowton, Springfield, Mass., at a time of flood in 1936; b, largest box of the family, standing a foot high; c, Shaker herb box; d, Colonist herb box.

one-half inches long, thirteen inches wide and seven inches deep. The cover has the same shaped lap, slender like a door hinge. A second box is very shallow and has a long pointed lap that extends around the box and is fastened with hand-made nails. The third one has a lap made of many points like a Shaker box, but the cover point turns in the opposite direction from the box points, and there are wooden pegs fastening the bottom and the top to their rims. These two characteristics show that the box is not one made by the Shakers. The two Shaker boxes are different in size — one is very deep, and the other is the largest in the nest of nine boxes, being fifteen inches long and ten and one-half inches wide.

The list of herbs is a long one. While today there are over three thousand different herbs that supply medical demands, even in the early days there were several hundreds. Some were picked for the seed, some for the blossom, some for the root, and still others for the stalk. Carroway was picked for the seeds, catnip had blossoms and leaves that were pressed, sage leaves were dried and ground and witch hazel was cut as a bush and dried, while the bark of sassa-fras was dried and powdered. Herbs were picked when the sap was running full, tied in bunches and dried. Hung from the rafters in the shed chamber or in the attic, they kept company with the seed corn. Some herb stalks were bent and pressed in short lengths while still green. After a season of drying the herbs were kept in the boxes. When they were to be used they were crushed and ground in mortars, and then sifted in the horsehair or silk mesh sieves. These powders were for medicinal purposes, but the "bitters and simples" that remain vividly in the minds of the older generations were made by brewing either the fresh herbs or those that had been dried.

Plate 84. Shaker herb tray, used
in carrying herbs from garden to
house. At right, a Shaker box
with handle.

The Shakers were the first in this country to use herbs
on a commercial basis, and by 1820 their medicine industry
was flourishing. The romance of herb lore, however, began
on these shores when the white man learned from the Indian
the healing and curing properties of certain plants.

In the collection is a rare Shaker tray in which herbs
were carried from the garden to the house or workshop.
It is twenty-four inches long, seventeen and one-half inches
wide and four and one-half inches deep, and fastened with
copper nails. It is painted that beautiful yellow called
pumpkin yellow while the inside part of the bottom is red
ochre.

The subject of paint in connection with antiques is an
important one and is discussed more fully in a later chapter.

On the wooden boxes, red, yellow, blue, green and gray paints are seen, and one is impressed with the soft beauty of these colors. Clay in the soil, called bog iron in many localities, was the foundation for the paint, and the natural colors were yellow, red and gray. The clay was crushed and powdered and mixed with white of eggs, skim milk or whey, to produce paint. The several colors of those early days were made by using dyes from vegetable growths.

BOXES FOR SUGAR AND MEALS

The boxes next smaller than the herb boxes were for

Plate 85. Group of odd handmade boxes for meal, sugar and spices. The small one at top was used by a shoe cobbler for his thread, which was passed through holes left by the removal of nails.

sugar and meal, and were both round and oval. Large quantities of sugar and meal were kept in barrels or tubs, and
only small quantities were kept in the boxes in the pantry.

The meals in those early years were corn meal (called
Indian meal), rye meal and oat meal. The meal from oats
was not known until later, however, and then only in certain localities. The Pilgrims learned from the Indians how
to plant and use corn, how to eat it green and how to make
the meal from the dried kernels. Had it not been for the
corn, the Pilgrims could not have lived through the first hard
years. Records speak of a corn brought from England,
but that was a species of wheat and not planted in the new
country to any great extent.

The principal dish of the Colonists was Indian meal pudding, which was served once and more often twice a day.
It went by the inconsistent name of hasty pudding, for it
was cooked in anything but a hasty manner. Mush was
another frequently heard name. Cakes made of Indian meal
and water were called bannock cakes and were similar to
the hoe cakes of the South; these were baked before the
fire on boards propped up with a skillet or kettle. Indian
meal mixed with rye meal, water and yeast made a finer
bread, which was baked in the brick ovens.

Meals were kept in barrels, and it was found that the
meal kept better when a large rock, the size of a pumpkin,
was put in the barrel. The rock prevented the meal from
lying too compactly together and also kept it at a cooler
temperature. These barrels were in the "butt'ry," and only
small quantities of meal were kept in the pantry in the boxes.

SALT BOXES

Occasionally a pantry box was used for salt, but the real
salt box is a four-sided box and belongs in the class of wall
boxes. Salt was kept near the heat of the fireplace, either in

a cupboard over the mantel shelf or on the shelf. A moisture, similar in appearance to that of sugar but greater in quantity, exudes from the salt and the stain always remains in the wood of the salt box, to return whenever there is any dampness in the air. One can thus readily detect a box that has been used for salt.

SOURCES OF SALT

At one time nearly all the salt used as food and for industrial purposes was obtained from sea-water, and if derived from this source, it was called "sea" or "bay" salt. The works were generally called salt gardens, consisting of a series of large, shallow, evaporating reservoirs. The salt water is admitted and flows slowly from one to another,

Plate 86. Another group of handmade oval boxes showing
fancy laps, handmade nails and different woods.

all the while evaporating under the heat of the sun, until finally the dry salt remains in crystalline crusts on the salting-tables in the last basins. The salt is raked up and sold just as it is formed, a very coarse salt, used for curing meats and for such purposes. This became an important business on Cape Cod after the Revolution. Salt was the earliest of manufactures in the new America; Jamestown, Virginia, established salt works in 1620 and sent salt to the Puritan settlers in 1633. Rock salt was found and excavated in West Virginia and in Louisiana.

The other great source of common salt is the vast mineral deposits. This mineral deposit is called rock-salt and is evidently the result of the evaporation of great shallow bodies of salt water in remote ages. This rock-salt is mined. In some localities water occurs naturally in the salt strata and the saturated brine is reached by deep borings; in other cases water is introduced into the borings and then pumped out again. After the brine is secured it is evaporated by artificial heat in large iron or copper vats.

Coming to the home in coarse form, salt was crushed in the mortar or later taken to the grist mill where it was ground between two large revolving, cylindrical stones. This grinding was done first by man power and later by water power. This quotation from 1834, referring to the labor-saving method, is amusing: "What expense this may save the dairy woman and the tired farmer when pestle and mortar must ring from morn till bedtime to pound a quart not so fine, but that it will grit like pigeon shot in your teeth."

The odd meal and sugar boxes, with individual laps, show much ingenuity and the artistic leanings on the part of the workers. They are of many sizes and depths and were constructed of plain and quartered oak, ash, and curly and bird's-eye maple, and were put together with hand-wrought nails.

SPICE BOXES

The spice boxes seem to be more numerous than any of the other boxes; the reason may lie in the fact that they are still often found in use. Some are round while others are oval, and again much ingenuity is shown in the way they are made. One has a long lap, extending around the box and caught with iron clamps, with a cover made in the same manner. One was sewed with fine wire, another fastened with shoe thread, and yet another with a strand of splint. One has no nails whatsoever. The lap was finished with two points which were tucked into two holes cut in the rim; even the cover lap has a point tucked into a hole.

Plate 87. a, b, Large round boxes showing odd laps and handmade nails; c, compass or gauge for marking out box covers and bottoms — lines can be seen on box cover; d, showing geometric pattern used in making oval cover; e, wall salt box.

Still another box has unusual workmanship; an ordinary lap in the box, but an exquisite locked-lap in the narrow rim of the cover. The spice boxes have more earmarks on them than the larger boxes.

Plate 88. A group of oval and a group of round spice boxes.

The first natural inclination is to open a spice box and smell the fragrance of the old spice, either the spice itself or the powder which still clings to the wood. If a box had at any time held cloves it will be found that the oil had penetrated the wood and left a rich, deep color which time has not destroyed. One box held a nutmeg grater which, being too big for the box, had made a groove in the box cover and in the bottom. In the same pantry where this box was found, were two boxes which had been badly charred in a tavern fire. The tavern was destroyed but the boxes had been rescued along with other kitchen treasures.

Jewelry was often kept in the small spice boxes. One box is lined with a piece of calico, while another has cotton in the bottom to protect the jewelry. A cobbler used a long narrow box for his spools of thread. He had pulled the nails from the lap of the box and ran his thread through the holes, after the manner of the industrious housewife who had her fancy sewing boxes.

Many boxes are labeled or dated in paint and often initials are found on them. Lacking paint, a sharp tool was used for this purpose. Figures showing business transactions are penciled on the inside of many covers, and one spells out the message to a six-year-old daughter, written nearly a century ago, "Be a good girl Roxy." Lettie I. Landers, in 1867, had an inspiration and wrote a poem on the inside of a large box. Unfortunately it cannot be made out, but it is about a "perfect day" and "think of the bride, friend girl cousin."

A spice box was used for a bee-hunting box, made with a hole in the cover over which was fastened a piece of glass. This was used in lining wild bees.

Maple was the common wood used in spice boxes. Some, however, are of birch, ash and beech, and an ornamental one was made of bird's-eye maple.

Spices are yet another imported article and were brought back on the trading vessels. The early nations, before Christ, discovered the preservative qualities of spices, and from then on, spices were used when storing food. Food that was heavily spiced kept over long periods, and as there were then no means of preserving food, as in modern times, it was a most important discovery. The Colonists pickled and spiced fish and game, vegetables and fruits and their wines and cordials

Plate 89. Set of eight spice boxes, each bearing label.

Food was prepared in large quantities in the fall of the year, and this carried the families through the long winters.

Spices were obtained from the bark, the roots and the fruits of plants. Cinnamon came from Ceylon. The trees are small cultivated trees that have no odor except when bruised, a leaf pulled off or a branch broken. The inner rind of the bark from the branches is stripped off, tied in bundles, dried in the sun and exported. Mustard is obtained from the sheaves of the stalks and the seeds of the mustard plant, dried and powdered. Cloves are blossoms, and allspice is the berry of the pimento, a tree of the West Indies. All-spice takes its name from the fact that it is supposed to contain the flavor of all the other spices. Mace is the cov-ering of the nutmeg, and pepper is the berry of a shrub. Ginger comes from the root of the ginger plant. These eight spices were found in the old nests of spice boxes — the round wooden nest and the oblong or round tin nest. Each box was labeled with its own spice and the cover of the

nest had s p i c e s painted in plain lettering. A wooden nest
is in the collection with six of the boxes full of the old spice.
The mace is not powdered but resembles dried sliced peaches
in color but like openwork.

An unusual piece in the collection, though not of wood,
is a jar of nutmegs. It is a three-quart, hand-blown jar,
filled with preserved nutmegs, which were sealed in alcohol
more than one hundred years ago. It was brought to this
country by a Captain Hoyt of Newburyport, Massachusetts,
on a return trip from the East Indies. The cover which sets
inside the jar was sealed with a rubber substance, and at
one time there was a leather covering that went over the
top of the bottle. Here is the whole fruit, which is much
like a peach in size and shape, the striped nutmeg stones and
the long slender leaves. It was a rare find for a collector interested in the early wooden ware and all that pertains to it.

Plate 90. Jar of nutmegs sealed in alcohol more than 100 years ago, showing the nutmeg, its covering of mace, and the leaves. Also a box which contained a nutmeg
grater when found, and a large grater nearly 180 years old.

Plate 91. Group of pill boxes.

PILL BOXES

The group of pill boxes is the smallest, numbering about three dozen. It shows both hand-made and factory-made boxes. Pine was used for these tiny boxes; the strip was held on the grindstone to produce a shell-like thinness which no knife could make. The laps were fastened with glue, because the wood was so delicate, and the top of the cover and the bottom were held in place by pressure of the rims. The smallest round one measures one and one-half inches in diameter, the oval one two by one and one-half inches.

The factory-made type of pill box has one small nail fastening the lap of the box, and another that of the cover, which is held in by pressure. The sizes range from one inch to three inches in diameter, and the larger of these have wooden pegs fastening the top and bottom to their respec-tive rims.

As has been said, the Shakers began the production of herbs for medicine about 1820. Lists tell us of the early pills as well as of the liquid products. Bottling, labeling and shipping of medicine grew to be a great industry, and accounts tell of exporting in large quantities to long dis-tances and at an early date.

[174]

The illustration shows a group of the pill boxes. Two of them, about seventy-five years old, have their labels still intact. One reads, "Dr. Phelps Compound Tomato Pills — Entirely vegetable — Price 37½ cents." On the side is the purchaser's safeguard, "None genuine without this label." The other box tells how the pills should be taken, "J. H. Schenk — dose from 4 to 6 pills." One tiny box has "eye stones" penciled on it. These stones are all but forgotten, used in curing an inflamed eye. A stone was put under the lid and allowed to move around, leaving a supposedly healing property as it came in contact with the eye ball.

An occasional small box is found which contained imported figs. These boxes are oval and made of cheap pine, poorly cut and roughly put together with machine-made nails. They cannot be prized in a collection of historical value as are the handmade products.

HINGHAM'S COOPERING INDUSTRIES

A history of Hingham, Massachusetts, mentions the fact that for two centuries following the settlement of the town in 1633, many coopering industries were thriving. This wooden ware was disposed of in exchange for corn, flour

Plate 92. Pie box, deep enough for two pies, one resting on the bottom of the box and the other on the frame which stands on four legs.

and other commodities. By 1840 the pieces were sold in unbroken lots, and the "Hingham bucket" became a necessity throughout New England. The history goes on to say that there were large and small tubs, the hoop and nest boxes, the "dumb-bettys," wash-tubs, keelers, piggins, etc. The hoop box was the butter box. Dumb-betty was a colloquial name and it must have been a wooden tray on which things were carried. Names sprang into existence with the making of different pieces, and only those who lived in certain localities could explain their meaning.

A keeler was a shallow, hooped tub which was used in cooling the milk. The piggin was a small bucket with a one-stave handle, in which food was carried to the pigs and which was used in catching the strippings of the cow when milking. The noggin was a wooden pitcher, handle and all made of one piece of wood. These articles are described and pictured in other chapters. From England came the names of losset or losad, meaning a wooden tray. A voider was a tray or basket for soiled dishes or for food. This turned into a butler's tray and was thought to have been made of splint.

In 1850 one Edmund Hersey of Hingham, Massachusetts, was making boxes by hand. Later, with the development of steam, he made his own machinery and prepared and sent to market one and one-half million strawberry, salt and fig boxes in a single year.

CHAPTER EIGHT

Buckets, Tubs and Kegs — The White Cooper Always
Found Trade Brisk

THE least artistic of the early wooden ware are the buckets, tubs and kegs. Built with only the thought of usefulness, they are strong and substantial. Much had to be carried, or toted as it was said, from house to barn, from house to town, to the fields to work and to the town to barter. Few of the old receptacles are left, for they gradually fell apart after such continuous hard usage.

The trade of making barrels, buckets, tubs and kegs dates back to 70 A. D. The man who made and repaired such staved pieces was called a cooper. There was the wet cooper and the dry cooper who respectively made barrels for liquids and for meals and sugar. The name white cooper was given to the man who made the smaller pieces, such as buckets, tubs, piggins, kegs for rum, water and powder, and the churns and canteens. In later years the traveling cooper journeyed from town to town each season and repaired these utensils in the home, taking with him his hand tools and materials to supply broken parts.

John Alden came into historical prominence through his romance with Priscilla as recorded in the poem by Longfellow, but few realize that he was a cooper, and but for that training he would not have been a passenger on the *Mayflower*. The ship's accommodations were filled, and for all his pleadings John Alden could not be accepted as a passenger. It was suggested that he be taken on as a cooper and this proved possible; so in that capacity John Alden came to these shores. On whaling vessels, the cooper's standing, or "lay," was next in order to that of an officer.

Every vessel setting sail had its cooper and the cruise often lasted two, three or more years.

THE GREASE BUCKET

The crudest and most unattractive piece of wooden ware is the grease bucket, or slush bucket, or tar bucket, as it was called in different localities. This is a small hollowed-out log, bound with riveted iron bands, and having a cover which sets into the opening. It has two extending ears with

Plate 93. Grease bucket made from a hollowed-out log.

holes through which a leather thong was strung and passed through a hole in the cover, back again through an opposite hole and an opposite ear, and then knotted. The thong was about two feet long and the cover slid up and down on it when it was used. Because of this arrangement the cover never went astray. There is a hole in the cover through which a stick was thrust into the mixture, and with this stick the hubs and axles were greased. Hanging from the rear axles, filled with pitch-pine, tar or slush, these grease buckets swung as the wagons jolted along. These wagons were sometimes the covered wagons that made long journeys to distant lands or that traveled back and forth to town, in those days often more than a day's journey. This grease bucket is an example of man's first wooden receptacle — a hollowed-out log. The details of it are clearly shown in the illustration, with the thong missing save for two short ends. If it could speak, this tar bucket might have endless tales to relate of the hardships and sufferings, the joys and happinesses that came to our ancestors as they courageously set forth to new country.

THE SUGAR BUCKET

As has been said of the boxes, buckets were first made at home as the necessity for such receptacles arose. A plane and other hand tools were all that were needed to make these small wares, and any handy man could keep his barn and kitchen supplied. Then it followed that some ambitious man would set up a shop in his home, in the shed or lean-to, or would build a shop out in the yard, and supply his neighbors and the villagers with buckets, tubs, kegs and other small staved pieces. So started the cooper shop.

The bucket most commonly seen is the sugar bucket with a cover and bale handle. Staves were cut of uniform length and made on a shave horse. A groove was cut near the end with a croze, into which the round, beveled-edged bottom was to be placed, as is explained in the portion on butter boxes. The bucket was made inside a tub, which had a raised, false bottom and an iron hoop ring about three-quarters of an inch high, which held the staves until a hoop was placed over them. These hoops were made first, the same size as the false bottom on which the bucket was built, and on the early buckets there were two hoops, one each at

Plate 94. Upper illustration shows three sugar buckets (covers missing) with as many different types of laps of hoops — two with locked laps, and the center one with the lapped hoops fastened with brads. Handmade nails were also used.

In lower illustration an extremely large sugar bucket is shown with handmade nails in lap and a forked lap in cover. In contrast to the large bucket is the miniature one of early factory period.

top and bottom, while later there were three, one at the top and two at the bottom. The staves were evened off with a leveler, and two holes were cut at opposite sides for the peg for the bale handle. The earliest type of peg was slipped through a hole at the end of the handle and then through a hole in the stave; then a small peg was driven into this peg so that it could not pull out. Another type of workmanship shows the peg cut off close on the inside of the bucket and a small piece of wood wedged into the split end — a method called splicing. The cover of the bucket was

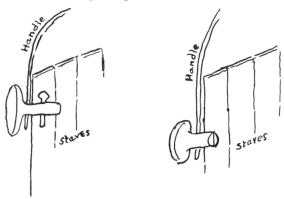

Plate 95. Showing cross section of pegs on bucket handles. One at left is pegged, one at right is spliced.

made like a box cover — it had a pine top and hickory or ash rim.

The hoops on these buckets show in what period the buckets were made. The first two types of hoops were called locked-lapped hoops, and a description and illustrations appear in Chapter Seven on boxes. The first lap had the arrow-shaped ends that were tucked under, and the next lap had the eyelet and shaped end, which was secured with a peg. These hoop fastenings show clearly in the illustration of the three sugar buckets, minus their covers. The third type of lap is factory-made with machine-made nail fastenings. The right-hand bucket is judged to be considerably over one hundred years old. The pegs holding the bale handle are fastened inside the bucket with a small peg. This type of fastening shows more clearly in the illustration of

[181]

the water buckets. The picture of the one sugar bucket shows a repair job on the handle. Evidently the peg came out and was lost. When a new one was made, the maker apparently became confused, as the head of the peg should be in reverse position. This is a very early bucket, its age being indicated by the locked-lapped hoops. Unfortunately the old coffin red with which it was first painted was covered with a nice new thick coat of gray. This "freshening-up" often breaks the heart of a collector. The large sugar bucket stands fifteen inches high, while in comparison the miniature bucket reaches only three inches. The large one is very old, with its lapped hoops and hand-forged nails, while the small one is factory-made.

The staves, bottom and cover of the sugar buckets are white odorless pine, for sugar was put in loose and would absorb any odor. The hoops and handle are of swamp ash or hickory, two woods which are pliable and have a resiliency necessary for bending. These hoops were made from the young sapling of the second growth of the tree, and the farmer called them hoop poles. If the hoops were to be left round and unfinished, very small saplings or branches were taken, sliced in two and used without much finishing. Sometimes the bark was left on.

WATER BUCKETS

Water buckets were made similar to the sugar buckets with the exception of protruding staves for the bale handle. These two staves allowed the bucket to stand away from the ground when it was turned over to dry. Water buckets had no cover. The hoops are strong and wide, and in some cases extended from top to bottom, making a re-enforced bucket. Of the six illustrated, all cooper products, two have locked laps, two tucked-under laps, and two lapped and

Plate 96. At top, group of water buckets showing the three types of laps. In the lower picture two buckets have hoops of hickory, one with bark left on. One in center has a hand-wrought iron ball handle. One at left retains original coffin red paint.

nailed laps, one of the latter having handmade nails and the other wooden pegs.

The dark small bucket with the iron handle is another rare type. A hand-wrought iron handle fastens into the two U-shaped projections of iron and is dainty in shape in contrast to the more unfinished type. The hoops are hickory

[183]

with the bark left on, and the tucked-under laps extend nearly halfway round the bucket. No one knows why it had an iron handle. Because the bucket still has an odor of tar, there is no doubt but what it was used on board ship. It was found in its present condition, filled with nuts, in an abandoned barn. Squirrels discovered the nuts and, in making a feast of them, had eaten through the staves, several of which are nearly gone.

A little bucket, standing five inches high and six inches in diameter, is one of the prize pieces of the collection. The two hoops were made from one small hickory branch, split in two and stripped of its bark. The bottom is penciled in an infirm hand, "1770 Made by E. Proctor when he was 10 years old." One can picture the small boy gathering eggs in his own bucket.

PIGGINS

The piggin is another member of the bucket family. It is small, averaging eight to ten inches in diameter, with one protruding stave for a handle, often eight inches long, with rounded end. As a man carried it, it hung at his side, his

Plate 97. Piggins. One at right may have been a sap bucket as well. The long stave handle is characteristic of a piggin.

hand grasping the handle from the inside. The name piggin is derived from a Scotch word meaning an earthenware pitcher, jar or pot. It was used in this country to catch the strippings at milking time, as a dipper for water and for carrying food to the hens or the little pigs. These old pieces never served one purpose alone — there were too many things in those days to be done.

SAP BUCKETS

The sap bucket had one short protruding stave for a handle, at the end of which was a hole. The bucket tapered

Plate 98. Sap bucket, sugar tub and spiles.

toward the top, instead of having straight sides like the water bucket. Sap buckets were crudely made for rough, out-of-door usage. The hoops were hickory saplings with the bark left on. The bucket hung by its short handle on the spiles which were driven into the maple trees. The early spiles were made of a piece of basswood or of sumach, with the pith burned out to make the hollow tube. Later spiles were made of tin.

[185]

Plate 99. Funnels used in transferring sap from buckets to sap carriers or kettles. Riveted iron hoops and hand-turned funnel.

SAP CARRIERS

The sap carriers were shaped like the sap buckets, but with two short, projecting staves. There was a hole in the end of each of the two staves and through these a stick was inserted. This stick acted as a carrier bar and the hook on the end of the shoulder yoke thongs hooked onto it at its center. With the aid of a yoke two sap carriers or two sap pails, similar to water buckets, could be carried at one time.

Plate 100. Two sap carriers from the collection of Mr. A. B. Wells of Southbridge, Mass.

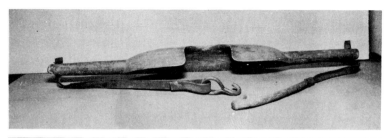

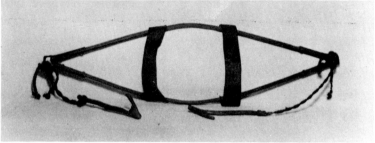

Plate 101. Shoulder yokes, at both ends of which leather thongs or cords of ropes were tied. Attached to these were hooks on which the sap carriers were hung. Lower one, style of Cape Cod Indians.

WELL BUCKETS

To withstand the constant out-of-doors exposure the well bucket was made as heavy and strong as possible. It had oak staves and riveted iron bands and an iron handle held by rings driven into a side stave. Many hoop bands were needed to make the staves secure and inasmuch as the staves bulged — had a "belly" — four hoops were placed at equal distances   The well buckets are seldom seen in use now, and most of them have long since fallen apart and been destroyed. The one pictured was found abandoned to spiders and their nests in a cellar of a country home.

The suction well bucket was an invention which was very little known. An iron lip was fastened with a leather hinge to the inside bottom of the bucket. When the bucket was lowered, the lip was forced open by the water and the bucket began to fill. When the bucket was raised, the lip

[187]

Plate 102. Well buckets, one equipped with a trap door.

closed with the pressure of the water, making the bucket water‑tight.

BUTTER CHURNS

It has been said that butter‑making was an oriental dis‑ covery, and may have come from the Arabs who carried milk in skin bottles on the backs of camels. The swinging movement of the animal in walking gave the necessary churning motion. Butter churns were first mentioned in America in 1644.

Butter churns were receptacles in which milk or cream was shaken or stirred to "break the outer skin of the butter globules, thereby enabling them to adhere closely together, in place of floating about independently in the liquid milk." The cream first "broke" in the churn and the butter col‑ lected in granular form. The buttermilk was then strained off and a small quantity of cool water put into the churn in place of the liquid drawn off. A second washing was done with plenty of water and a little salt, to cool and con‑ solidate the butter. A third time a small quantity of water was added, just enough to float the butter so that it might be more easily removed from the churn. The butter was then placed in wooden trays or in the various types of

[188]

Plate 103. Three early butter churns. The plungers of two are missing. The small one, built like a tankard. was loaned for the picture.

butter-workers so that the water could be pressed out. Salt was added at that last working, unless fresh butter was desired. If for various reasons the butter was of a pale color, carrot juice was added; but butter did not keep long with this coloring matter in it.

Butter churns vary in their construction, although the one most commonly known is the staved and hooped, high and slender tub. These have a cover which is set into the churn, with a hole in it through which the plunger is worked. The plunger is merely a long handle with crossed pieces of wood at the end with a hole in each of the four ends.

Pump churns were equipped with a pump which was worked by an arm acting as a fulcrum, moving the plunger up and down. The dasher on these pump churns was more elaborate; it consisted of two paddles each with many holes through which the cream flowed. The pump churn pictured

Plate 104. Pump churn of a factory period, painted "wagon wheel" blue.

was made box-like and painted the delightful wagon-wheel blue. Although many of these, made exactly alike, are to be found, they are not a factory product. Such articles made by factories have a patent stamp on them.

Another type of churn — and it is most primitive — is the rocking churn, so called because it was equipped with rockers. There are many of these in varying styles and sizes, made by the man of the house, possibly at the request of his wife. These churns could be rocked either by handles on the top or by treading on the rockers. It would seem that the busy housewife could work with her hands at knitting or mending while she rocked the churn with her feet. Inside of the churn were partitions, perforated with holes, through which the cream poured and which acted like the dashers of the other churns.

A still different type of churn is the barrel churn which could be run by horsepower if made on a large enough scale. This was a barrel set up on a frame, having a crank which turned the perforated boards inside. Large barrels facilitated the work of butter-making by churning large quantities at one time.

A factory-made churn is the round one standing on a flat base — in the shape of a drum. The working part inside consists of three or four paddles, turned by a crank on the outside. An opening at the top through which the cream was poured is clamped down tight with metal fasteners.

Plate 105. Small factory-period churn with paddle and crank.

This stood on a rack or table while the butter was being made.

All the necessary equipment for making butter is in the collection. First there is the skimmer which took the cream from the "setting" milk. Then there is the yellow sour-cream tub, a dilapidated, much-used affair, in which the cream stood until there was enough to make a batch of butter.

There is a beautiful scoop, stained and varnished, for removing the butter from the churn, although many house-wives used their hands, first washed in cold water, for this purpose, saying it made the task simpler. Then there were the bowls into which the butter was placed for working out the water by means of butter workers (Plate 36).

A butter worker on a large scale consists of a frame, fan-shape, three feet long and eighteen inches wide at the front and a foot wide at the back. In it is a roller, sometimes smooth and as often corrugated, with a handle. The oppo-site end of the roller fitted into a slot at the narrow part of the frame. The roller was rolled back and forth to work out the water, which trickled out the hole at the end of the frame. This frame was placed on a table while the operation was going on and a tub stood under one end to catch the liquid. (Plate 35) The butter was salted and often colored.

The butter was then ready for the tubs and boxes or for making into molds. "Scotch hands," narrow corrugated machine-made paddles, shaped the butter into pats. (Plate 37) From the time the milk was poured into the keeler, or an earthen bowl, until the butter was ready to be eaten, the process was a particular one.

TANKARDS

Similar in construction to the small churn is the tankard of staves and hoops (Plate 22). The staves, bottom and cover are pine, and the hoops, three or four in a group, are lapped hickory withes with the bark left on. The artisti-cally-shaped handle is cut all-in-one with a stave and has no fastening except for the hoops, which hold in the staves.

[192]

The cover is pegged to the handle, having a slot which fits around the top part of the handle.

Webster says a tankard is "a large drinking vessel, especially one with a cover." It held cider, wines, toddy or flip. The hot iron toddy stick, or the flip dog or loggerhead as it was called, was plunged into the tankard to heat the drink and give it a pleasant temperature. The iron toddy stick hung by the fire and was thrust into the embers when the drinks were being mixed. The heated iron added a burnt taste to the drink. Some pairs of andirons were fashioned with a holder for a cup at the top of the two standards, and had a rod across the two at the bottom on which to rest the feet, and an iron across the top to be used as a toddy stick. The toddy stick of wood was kept on the shelf or in a small cupboard over the fireplace. This could never have been very hot.

The flip glass was a large handleless mug of thin glass in which the flip was made. The flip consisted of spirits, hot water, lemon, sugar, and an egg if it was desired. This was stirred and mashed with toddy sticks which were slender sticks having a head at the end with which to mash. These are often mistaken for the spinning-wheel drivers, but those used for spinning have a very small end and they show wear at the head where they caught the spokes of the wheel. There is more variety in the toddy sticks than in the drivers. Sometimes a flat spoon was made for a stirrer for toddy (Plate 51).

The Pilgrims did not use water as a drink. The new land afforded little chance for good sanitation for many years, and a statement that Governor Bradford found water a "pleasant drink" indicates that it was little used. Even bathing in water was not generally practiced, and it was as late as the beginning of the nineteenth century before a bath tub was known. So drinks were made and served at the table and fireside and taken into the fields. The tankard and the flip glass were always near at hand and the iron toddy sticks were heating in the embers many times a day. Strangers and friends alike were greeted with a friendly drink at the fireside.

A small syrup jug, made like the tankard with staves and hoops, was a rare find. This could have been used for flip or toddy as well as the large tankards. The tiny nose of this small jug was fashioned from one of the staves, and the cover follows the curve of the nose. The bottom edge of the staves is cut in points and this fact causes one to think the jug could not slip or tip over as it might have done were it smooth. The jug began life in Worcester County, Massachusetts, went to Cape Cod, was found by a dealer, and then ended its travels in my home in Worcester. It was recognized by its original owners when seen in an exhibit of mine. Who can tell of the wanderings of this wooden ware — in covered wagon, by horseback, and by horse and buggy! (Plate 22)

KEGS

The kegs were made by the white cooper and were similar to buckets, except that the two ends were sealed. There were water kegs, rum kegs, powder kegs, the swigler, canteens and oyster kegs. These kegs are scarce for, as they contained water or other liquid, the wood deteriorated and repair was impossible after any length of time. The staves were grooved for the heads just as in the butter boxes and buckets, and they were locked securely by the hoops, which allowed for expansion and contraction. Some of the kegs were made with a raised bung hole; the middle part of one of the staves was left thicker than the ends so that the hole would not split the wood. The early kegs have wooden plugs. The water keg was made of oak staves and had iron bands and an iron handle, like the well bucket. These have pewter bung holes.

Plate 106. Water kegs. The two at right were soldier canteens, while the one at the left was used in taking water to the fields. The straps for carrying are missing.

RUM KEGS

The rum kegs were called "rundlets," from an old word meaning a measure now equal to eighteen gallons. The heads of the kegs are nearly triangular in shape and the locked laps of ash are bent to fit. The wood is pine and the kegs are very light in weight. On one that is pictured the original

Plate 107. Rundlets, or rum kegs.

Plate 108. Rum keg with three small swiglers. At right is a powder keg.

cord is still fastened and the stopper is intact, while the smaller keg has a wire bent through the holes for a handle. These kegs for water and rum were taken to the field when the men went to work. Rum found its way to America soon after the Colonies were founded, for trade was opened early with Jamaica and the West Indies. Wood was shipped in exchange for rum, slaves, and the various spices which the new country did not have.

Plate 109. Rum keg in perfect condition; at right, oyster keg with wide opening.

The powder kegs are barrel-shaped kegs and were carried by a wire handle. They seem to have been of the same standard size.

SWIGLERS

The small keg, cylindrical in shape and eight by four inches, or even smaller, was called a swigler. It was just what the name implied — a small keg that held a swig. They were made of a hollowed-out piece of wood with the two heads driven in when the wood was dry. When it was wet, the heads expanded to fit the opening and became water-tight. One small swigler was made of alternating light and dark wood, one wood dovetailed within the other. Four copper bands are riveted around the keg and the bung hole is the raised part of a stave.

OYSTER KEGS

The oyster keg is a crude affair, unfinished and of poorly chosen wood. The keg stands ten inches high and the opening is the size of a large oyster. These kegs were made and used only in sections where oysters were found. The keg is of the same type of crude, hasty workmanship as the clam basket of splint. Perhaps these were of a later date, but they both show hand work.

CANTEENS

The two canteens pictured were flasks for water for the soldier in war. The small canteens date from the war of 1776 and were made by hand. The rim of ash is sewed with coarse thread, and two narrow leather straps were once fastened on either side of the bung hole, through which a longer strap was inserted and by which the flask was carried.

Plate 110. Two upper illustrations are wash tubs showing two types of hoops. The larger tub was constructed of both sap wood and heart wood, showing contrasting colors. The lower tub, though of wash tub type, is said to have been used in making bread.

The large canteen resembles a mouse trap in appearance and has the leather straps intact. This is very sturdily made of ash and pine and heavy nails and, filled with water, would hold at least two quarts. It must have been a burden to any soldier. Initials and dates are often found on these canteens, recording the person to whom it belonged and the war in which it saw service. Some of these round canteens were carried into the fields for the day's labor.

TUBS AND KEELERS

Tubs were staved and hooped like buckets and had two protruding, short stave handles with handle holes. These tubs were made by a cooper before factories found their way into villages. There were foot tubs for the family, tubs for dishwashing and tubs in which the clothes were washed. The tubs were both round and oval and had both wooden and iron hoops. The largest tub in the collection was rescued from a wood pile in the country. It is nearly three feet in

Plate 111. Round keeler, showing early hoops.

diameter and eighteen inches deep. In the smallest tub the staves were dowelled, a manner unusual in tubs. In another tub the staves were made from both sap wood and heart wood and the contrasting color shows in the picture.

[199]

The keeler is a shallow, hooped tub, either round or oval. The protruding stave-handles are high in proportion to the depth of the tub. Two locked hoops cover the staves from the bottom to the top edge. The keeler may be confused with a tub, but the difference lies in the depth, the keeler being more shallow. The name keeler comes from the German word *kiel,* meaning to cool. Milk was poured into the

Plate 112. Keeler at Hingham Historical Society, Hingham, Mass. Two gauges, with pencil in one end and a nail point in the other, used in marking bottoms of boxes and tubs.

keeler at milking time so that it might cool, the shallowness of the tub hastening this process. The keeler was also used when butter was washed with cold water after it was taken from the churn.

Keelers are a very old type of receptacle and little is known of their history. The first ones originating in Europe were made by hollowing out a shaped, thick slab of oak. Keelers appear in many old paintings of home scenes.

SUGAR   TUBS

The maple sugar industry supported many families; the sugar orchards were the source of most of the sugar and the so-called molasses used in those early years.

Plate 113. Two small sugar tubs.

The sugar tubs are the large well-made tubs with locked-lapped hoops and a cover with a deep rim. As was stated in Chapter Five, there were two types of tubs, one for the soft sugar and one for the wrapped cakes of sugar.

Plate 114. Sugar tub used for cakes (cover missing). The wet sugar required a tub with a plug near the bottom out of which the sugar molasses was drawn.

Plate 115. Dye tub and a sour cream tub with a set-in cover.

A letter from an elderly friend who was brought up on a farm in New England is well worth quoting. It gives a happy, vivid picture of sap gathering:

"I grew up on a large farm where several hundreds of pounds of maple sugar were sold annually, and was a member of my Grandfather's household for several years, watching the activities and helping with the 'sugaring' until I was sixteen years old. My Grandmother never used any sugar except maple, excepting a small package of confectioner's sugar which was used only to frost the cake for the minister's donation each fall. Her sugar bowls were filled with the finest maple, as light in color as the light brown sugar we use now for dark cake and mince meat. The early run of sap was cooked to the right consistency and partially cooled, being stirred very little so as not to break the grain, and poured at just the right minute into a long box-like trough with little partitions about every eight inches. The partitions were lifted carefully out after the sugar cakes were hard and these cakes were stored on clean boards or tin trays, upstairs in a dry spot, until thoroughly dry. Then they were taken to market or packed in tubs for family use.

"The late runs of sap made darker sugar, which was poured into tubs, and when cold the stopper was taken from a hole in or near the bottom of the tub and a dish left under it to catch the slowly dripping syrup of maple molasses until no more would form. This dark stuff was used for brown bread or mince meat, not just to be thrifty and

[202]

saving, but it was done that way to make the sugar dryer and lighter in color. It was stored upstairs where it was dry (it would have a thin filmy mold over it otherwise), and was called soft sugar and dug out from the top of the tub as needed. The stopper or plug (a whittled stick) was put back into the hole to keep out the ants and flies and the cover put on or a clean cloth tied over the top. I have helped with every move in the work of sap gathering from boring the holes in the trees to washing out the sap buckets, drying them in the sun and storing them away under the roof of the old sugar-house. Then on the way back to the house I have looked in the warm hollows and found spring beauties and dog-tooth violets to carry home to my Mother, sometimes hearing the first robin or bluebird on the way. It is all so vivid and sweet to remember. I wouldn't ask to be 'brought up' anywhere but on a farm."

ODD TUBS

There were tubs for large quantities of butter, standing seventeen or eighteen inches high and tapering toward the

Plate 116. Butter tub, paddle and a small tub used in taking butter out to the fields.

top. In the illustration there is a paddle lying near the tub with which the butter was packed in or taken out. The little tub in the group has been called both a salt tub and

Plate 117. Octagon candy pail with mitered edges.

a butter tub. It was made for taking butter out into the fields for the day's work and is said to have come from Sweden. Many early tools and receptacles used in this country came from across the water.

A lye tub was a small-sized tub which was used to catch the lye as it dripped from the leach barrel. Lye for soap was obtained by soaking birch ashes in water. The ashes which accumulated during the winter were put into a barrel, filling it about two-thirds full, leaving the rest of the space for water. The barrel rested on a lye stone which was cut with a channel, into which the lye ran and from which it trickled into a lye tub.

The dye tub was a covered tub used for holding the dye when dying materials. The dyes were made in big iron kettles and then poured into the tub. (The method of obtaining color is explained in Chapter Eleven.) This tub stood at one side of the fireplace and was used as a seat. Many a lover proclaimed his love seated on the tub and woe to him if the tub overturned. It was a never-forgotten accident according to the accounts of the old days, both because of the stain and the odor.

The most popular dye was the blue taken from the Indigo plant. This plant was first brought from India on whaling vessels and also from Africa. But a wild plant was discovered in the Colonies and this gave twenty times as much coloring matter. The leaves were pounded while green in mortars and reduced to a pulp which was formed into thick round cakes or balls. These were dried and kept until needed for dyeing. Or again the leaves were powdered with the

Plate 118. Complete set of letters used in stamping names on buckets, tubs and boxes. Bucket used for corn kernels.

lye of wood ashes. Children picked the leaves of the wild American plant at three cents a pound.

The largest tubs of all were those in which hogs were scalded. This operation was done out in the yard. It called for two skilled men, pulleys, ropes, a tub, a hog and a hog scraper. As an old settler said, "It was a gory operation."

A still different tub or pail was called a kit. This was smaller at the top than at the bottom and was used for butter and for fish. Later mills putting out these tubs were called kit mills.

Plate 118a. Three tubs for carrying butter to the fields. The one at the right was carved out of one piece of wood. The cover is fastened by means of the rope and it slides up, but not off. The cord to the middle one is missing.

Plate 118b. Two Shaker apple butter buckets.

CHAPTER NINE

*Sieves — From the Tiny Sieve for Medicine Powders
to the Large Charcoal Sieve*

S IEVES were very important in long-ago days, as many
things, such as sugar, salt, herbs, spices, soda and
meals, were ground, crushed and sifted before they
could be used. Grandma in the kitchen and grandpa in the
barn both had their sieves. Whether made of hair or of splint
these sieves were works of art, and perhaps the finest examples of handwork found in any of the wooden ware.

SIEVES OF HAIR

The earliest type of sieve found in the old New England
homes was made of hair — reds, browns, grays and black —
taken from horses' manes and cows' tails. The hair was
sorted and tied in bundles of several lengths, according to
the size of the sieve to be made. The hoops were of ash or
quartered oak, like those of the pantry boxes, made either
in graded sets or in the regulation size of twelve inches.
Each sieve had two hoops, one fitting into the other. The
mat was woven, the edges sewed over and over with a
coarse thread and clamped between the two hoops. Nails
held it securely in the rims, so taut and even that after
many years of use the mats are still firm.

LOOM FOR MAKING SIEVE MATS

In the Old Hadley Museum situated in Old Hadley, Massachusetts, there is a loom on which mats for sieves were
woven. It stands about five feet high and is eighteen inches
wide, and was operated from a high stool. With it are
bundles of black hair in different lengths, a finished mat
and a few hoops — silent memorials of labor performed
many years ago.

Plate 119. At top is shown an unusual sieve with several shades of horsehair. Sieve at left has a mat bound with a bias binding of calico before it was clamped into the two hoops. Second view from top shows the five sieves in front row that were used in a doctor's office. Third illustration from top shows some double-covered sieves. The oval one has a horsehair mat, while the round one has a thin gauze mat. At bottom is an unusual winnowing sieve of quartered oak showing method of fastening ends on inside of rim.

This loom was originally owned by two sisters, Hattie and Sarah Marsh, who lived in the village of Old Hadley. They were the third generation to live in the house which had been built by their grandfather. Spinsters in the true sense of the word, they were very eccentric and remained indoors constantly, with the blinds drawn. A brother lived with them and attended to any contacts necessary with the outside world. The sisters made and sold sieves as a means of livelihood.

SHAKER SIEVES

Records of Shaker Colonies state that sieve-making became an important industry beginning in 1810 in the colony at New Lebanon, New York. Those early records list "hare sives" and "waer sives." In the Shaker Collection in the New York State Museum in Albany there are sieves and a sieve-binder, showing the method of binding the mats. This sieve-binder is a three-legged stool of working height, with the top the size of a sieve, flat with straight sides. A cover of sheet iron with a rim of lead fits the top of the stool. After the mat was woven, it was placed on the binder, the cover pressed firmly down, and the edge sewed over and over with a coarse thread. The bound mat was then clamped between the two hoops and fastened with very small nails.

A crudely-made sieve, twelve inches in diameter, has a mat which was sewed over and over and then bound with a bias piece of homespun. The fine stitches show that it was made with great care, and further handwork appears in a darn which fills a break caused by hard usage. The sieve hung by a piece of calico strung through a square hole in the rim.

Sieves made of pierced calfskin and goatskin have been found but these would give good service only as long as the leather did not dry and crack.

Plate 120. Loom for weaving horsehair mats for sieves. (In the Old Hadley Museum at Old Hadley, Mass.) Inset shows horsehair tied in bundles of different lengths, hoop and a finished mat found with the loom.

SIEVES OF SILK AND OF WIRE

An extremely fine white silk was woven into mats for the small sieves used in sifting medicinal powders. This was called bolting cloth — from bolting, meaning to sift. In the collection there is a set of five round sieves from two to six inches in diameter, at one time in use in a doctor's office. The herb powders still cling to the edges of the mesh. Three of these sieves are of white silk, one of black-and-white horse-hair and the other of extremely fine wire. Another nest has one mat of the silk and two of hair.

The Shakers made and sold what they called "riddles." These were sieves with a mat of brass wire, used for wheat and for seeds. Wire in sieves did not appear for general use until many years after horsehair had been used. My "adopted grandmother" said that when her father brought home their first wire sieve there was much rejoicing. It made sifting much easier. One can readily see how difficult it must have been to sift with the closely-woven hair sieves.

DOUBLE-COVERED SIEVES

Double-covered sieves apparently were not considered any improvement over the ordinary sieves, for they are seldom found. They had two covers, one for the top and one for the bottom and appear to have been made by the Shakers and used for sifting seeds. They are oval in shape, seven inches long, four inches wide and six inches deep. Enclosed like a box, the double-cover arrangement prevented the seeds from scattering as they were being sifted. When the oval sieve shown in the illustration was found, there were tiny husks of a seed in the hair mesh, but these disappeared as curious ones smoothed the mesh with their fingers.

During the first year of my research work I went to a museum in Boston for a conference with the curator. I was asked to name and describe the small collection of Shaker wooden ware which the museum owned. On the shelves, where lay some of the few sieves, were found many tiny particles which appeared to be parts of moth millers in a dried stage. The curator called lustily for his secretary to bring camphor balls. Two years later, similar shell-like particles were discovered in my covered sieve, and were found to be the husks of an herb seed!

There is a round double-covered sieve which shows clumsy handwork and appears to have been made by a settler, while the oval, accurately-made ones are Shaker products. This round one has large, handmade nails in the fastenings; the mesh of the sieve is a thin black gauze, not bound, but clamped in in an unfinished manner. As would be expected, the mesh did not hold and the sieve was finally used as a box for everything and anything. Stains from berries are on one cover and the other cover shows knife marks.

WINNOWING SIEVES OF SPLINT

For sifting grain a heavy sieve was used, made of splint, and called a winnowing sieve. After the grain was cut it was taken to the barn and spread on the floor, where it was beaten with flails to separate the kernels from the chaff. A flail was a long wooden handle with a shorter piece of wood fastened to it by means of leather ties. After this beating, the grain was put into a winnowing basket and tossed up and down to free the kernels from the chaff. Winnowing baskets were made of wood or splint in the shape of a large ellipse, as long as the span of a man's reach. They look like large scoops with a rim at the back on which are two handles

by which the basket was held. In Pennsylvania, there were winnowing floors made with planks set far enough apart so that the grain might fall through. The winnowing baskets were also called bolters or bolts which was another name for sieves.

After the grain was tossed in the winnowing baskets, it was sifted in the winnowing sieves. Several of these are in the collection and each one shows different workmanship, according to the skill of the creator. One is thought to be a Shaker product, it being so perfectly made. A rim of quartered oak, measuring twenty inches

Plate 121. Flail for threshing grain. Consists of a long handle to which is fastened a stick which swings from a leather and rope cord. Handle is over three feet in length.

[212]

in diameter and six inches wide, is fastened with handmade nails, and the mat is of ash splint, narrow and most evenly cut. To fasten the mat onto the rim, two rows of holes were bored at the edge of the rim, an inch apart, in a curve, eight curves around the rim. This was done so that the rim would not split. In one sieve the holes were bored in a straight line with the grain of the wood and the rim split. Eight metal clamps were used to repair the damage

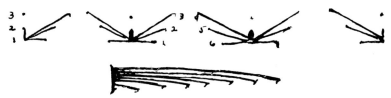

Plate 122. Manner of fastening the splint in a winnowing sieve. The ends resemble a butterfly. The lower fastening resembles a wing.

caused by poor planning. In the Shaker sieve a strand of splint was threaded through one hole and out the corresponding hole in the line above, and then cut off. This was done when the splint was wet and pliable. (Plate 129)

One sieve with an ash hoop appears to be older than the Shaker sieve. The holes for the splint were again cut in a curve, each curve having six holes. Three extra holes, one above the other, were bored between the curves. As the splint was threaded through the six holes, three of the ends were caught with three from the next set of six, cut off and fastened with a seventh strand. This strand was threaded through the lowest of the three extra holes, back through the middle one, out through the top one, and cut off. Looking at the strands on the inside of the rim one sees a fastening resembling a butterfly.

The most beautiful workmanship of all the sieves is found in the one which has a quartered oak rim, and the splint is threaded through slits instead of bored holes. The weaving

[213]

was done in a group of eight. Seven strands were tucked into seven slits and the seven ends were brought to one point and cut off. These ends were then fastened with an eighth strand. In between each group of eight slits, two slits were cut which held the fastening. The eighth strand was threaded through one slit and out the other and then cut off close, holding the seven ends securely. This fastening resembles a wing and shows in the illustration. (Plate 119)

CHARCOAL SIEVES OF SPLINT

In the early days the only known coal was charcoal. Besides being used for fuel it was used in medicines, in polish and as a fertilizer. Making charcoal was an industry which was carried on in many sections and which required skill, and often as many as 5,000 cords of wood were cut. Sometimes a pit was dug in which the wood was stacked, but as often as not it was stacked on the ground. Birch or maple was used — birch because it smoldered without burning too hard, and maple because it was a solid pure wood with a clean ash. There were two ways to stack the sticks. They were laid cobhouse fashion as were the sticks of the wooden chimneys, or they were stood up and brought to a point like tepee poles. They stood higher than a man. Thick sods were then packed solidly over the structure, completely covering it. Sometimes clay was used if it was easily obtained. A small hole was left in the side of the casing so that a draft might be created and through which the worker might watch the smoldering sticks. Great care was taken that the fire did not grow to a flame; the process was simply intended to char the wood. It took about three days and three nights and required constant attention. When the wood was all charred, the sticks crumbled and fell down within the casing. The sods, or clay, were lifted off and the charred sticks taken away in barrels to a shed where the process of sifting and sorting was done. Charcoal that was made from wood growing in sandy soils, which wood turners found turned the edge of their tools, made fine powder for polishing.

Charcoal sieves are about two feet square and they have a depth of six inches. Oak rims support the upper edge, and eight supports, four each way, are woven across the bottom. The splint is one inch or more wide. The sides were woven solid and there are holes in the bottom made by the weaving, half an inch square. The sieve was built solidly to hold the weight of the charcoal. The sifting separated the large pieces from the fine dust.

Following the making of sieves by hand, factories with machinery began to manufacture sieves in large quantities. Grain was harvested by machinery and taken directly from the fields, through the mills, to the consumer. This progress of achievement soon did away with the hand products. Wire sieves of today have no particular interest for us.

Plate 122a. Hatchel for straightening hair -- cows' tails, horses' tails and horses' manes. The platform above screwed down to hold the hair.

CHAPTER TEN

Splint Found in the Early Wooden Ware —
How Obtained and How Used

No ONE knows when splint was first made. It seems
to be one of those things that has been used for
generations and the art of using it handed down
from father to son. Without doubt the Indians had been
making splint for years when the white man came to these
shores. The research student rarely knows just how one
race or generation learns from another race or generation.
Do they actually sit with them and watch? Or do they
examine what has been done and either copy it or improve
upon it? The white man, in all probability, watched the
Indian and then, with greater creative powers, ventured
further.

The white man was supplied with many luxuries with
which the Indian was unfamiliar. Bartering, or exchanging,
was the only way by which these commodities could be had,
and baskets figured frequently in such transactions.

INDIANS' SPLINT

The Indians made splint from the ash tree and the white
oak. The wood of those two trees, particularly the second
growth, was tough, porous and flexible.

The Indian felled the tree in the early spring when the
sap had begun to flow freely. The bark was peeled off, and
the log allowed to lie several weeks to weather. The wood
was then pounded with a wooden mallet. This pounding
loosened the wood which was then stripped off in splinters,
the entire length of the tree. These strips were then bound
together with birch or hickory withes, weighted and sub-
merged in a pond or brook, to stay until used. When the

Indian needed a basket, he helped himself to the splint, stripped the splinters into the widths he wanted, and set to his task. Reeds and rushes were used in making fancy baskets, but the splint basket was severely plain, round, square or oblong. The Indians often painted little flower designs on the splint baskets with berry juices.

A later way to make splint was to quarter the tree and split the strips off from the cross sections. This made what was called quartered grain. The quartered pieces were placed on a riving horse and split into strips, the full length of the section, two inches wide and three inches thick. This was done with a hand knife or a riving chisel driven into the wood with a beetle. To rive means to split. These strips, called rivings, were then pounded with this same beetle and split with the grain of the wood into splits about half an inch thick. The next step was to put them on to a shave horse and smooth them. Then they were ready to be split into desired widths for various uses. This was done by adjusting two knives in clamps, between which the splits, as they were then called, were drawn. This was called a "hand-stripper." The finished strips were put back into the brook until needed.

All of the early splint was either ash or white oak. Hickory was used later and the Shakers used it exclusively beginning about 1800. This fact helps to place the age of splint pieces, especially chair seats.

A local invention called a steam box was made later which did away with soaking splint in water. This consisted of two boxes; one was a copper tank with a compartment underneath for a fire and the other was equipped with shoes or supports which held the splint. Pipes connected the two boxes, carrying the steam from the water in the copper tank to the splint.

The white man made much use of splint. There are cheese baskets, ox muzzles, clam baskets, apple-drying baskets, fish baskets, charcoal sieves, winnowing baskets and winnowing sieves, and many utility baskets. Countless chair seats also were of splint.

WEAVING SPLINT

The hexagon weaving of the cheese basket was the strong-est of all types, with never any slipping of the splint. Two strands, commonly about three-quarters of an inch wide, were crossed. A third strand was set in the upper crotch of the crossed strands and a fourth set in the lower crotch.

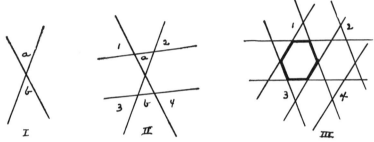

Plate 123. Hexagon weaving in cheese baskets — I, two crossed splints; II, two strands set into crotches a and b, making four crotches; III, strands of splint set into each crotch 1, 2, 3 and 4, forming a hexagon.

This made more crossed strands into each of which a strand was set, until the mat was the desired size for the bottom of the basket. Then the strands were turned up and the same manner of weaving continued. The bottom was in the shape of a hexagon because the weaving made hexagonal holes. When the desired depth of the basket was reached the splits were cut off at a point three or four inches beyond this depth, the ends were trimmed on a slant and bent back and tucked into the weaving alternately, one in and one out. Two hoops, either hickory or ash, were used for the edge. The one for the outside was shaped, curved on one side and flat

[218]

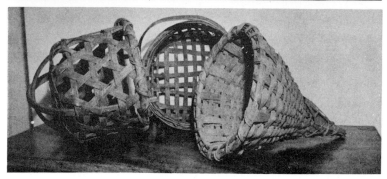

Plate 124. Three cheese baskets at top show hexagon weaving and the bound edge. Center illustration shows at left a utility basket with solid sides and with handles. At right, an egg basket, and in front another cheese basket. At bottom is an ox muzzle, a clam basket and a large funnel, examples of skilful weaving.

on the other, while the inside hoop was a flat strip. These were laced on with two strands of splint, one crossing the other, making a very strong, firm edge. All of this was done while the splint was wet and pliable. As it dried, it shrank and became tight. The cheese basket is fairly common in comparison with the other articles of splint.

Sometimes when weaving splint baskets a pattern was marked on the floor of the shed with chalk. Then the bottom was made by laying the pieces of splint on the pattern. There were molds, too, on which the weaving was done. There were shaped wooden blocks, sometimes made on a standard, but more often used on a table. They were similar to hat molds or blocks which were made of plaster of Paris as well as of wood. But in the early years all the weaving was done in the lap, with no guide.

OX MUZZLE

The ox muzzle in the collection was woven in the hexagon pattern. Two supports were set over the bottom, ending at the upper edge, to prevent the ox from pushing its tongue through the holes to eat grass. Other muzzles were woven solid, in a long slender shape.

The egg basket pictured and other utility baskets were also woven in the hexagon pattern. This pattern was optional; it took less splint, but more skill.

VINEGAR FUNNEL

The rarest piece of splint in the collection is the large funnel which was used in transferring vinegar. This was probably made on a mold. The funnel measures eighteen inches long and its opening is thirteen inches in diameter. Each split which starts from the point was cut like an arrow head, seven inches long. These ends are free, allowing for expansion when in use, and the weaving (that is, the filling) begins above the arrow-head points. The fills are narrow at the starting point and wide at the opening, and the weaving is solid. The support splits, which make the frame, are tapered for a distance of five inches beyond the rim of the funnel, then turned back and tucked under the cross splits, every other one turned inside and the alternating ones outside. Like the cheese basket, two hickory hoops are bound on to the edge, but with only one lacing of splint. To keep the arrow-shaped points from breaking, a thin strip of splint was laced around them and caught up in the sides. It was expertly planned and beautifully woven. In the course of years the point of the funnel closed. When used as a funnel, cheesecloth was placed inside.

CLAM BASKET

The clam basket is a very crude affair, woven with only the idea of usefulness. The splint is heavy and the weaving is irregular. The bottom of the basket was made square, with square corners; then at a depth of seven inches it was finished round, with two hickory hoops nailed on to the edge. There is no nice job on this basket of turning back the ends and binding on the hoops; the hand-cut nails, however, tell that it is old. A hickory handle swings on a tin support nailed to the rim. This basket probably originated on Cape Cod where clams are found.

APPLE-DRYING BASKETS

A few apple-drying baskets are still in existence and they show much individual planning. One resembles a stretcher, made of sticks running lengthwise with splint-weaving crosswise. This was used indoors. Four long hooks were fastened in the ceiling in front of the fire. Two sticks were laid crosswise on the hooks, and on these sticks the rack was

[221]

laid. Often such hooks are still seen in the old kitchens, where long ago the sliced apples dried.

A cobweb drier is just what the name implies — a rack built like a cobweb. The ribs are hickory sticks and the fills are of splint, woven openly as the spider spins its web. This

Plate 125. A cobweb apple drier which suspends from the ceiling by its center rod. (Photo by Mr. Howard G. Hubbard, former curator of Skinner's Museum, South Hadley, Mass.)

rack, filled with the slices of apples and hung by the center, was spun around by the heat from the fireplace. The owner will not part with the rack and, like many other treasures, it cannot be bought.

The long splint basket was used on the window sill and the slices of apples dried out in the sunshine. This basket is four feet long, two feet wide, and has a depth of seven inches. The splints have no uniform width, varying from two inches to less than one inch, and they are woven with about an inch spacing. The edge is finished like the other splint baskets, but unfortunately only one strand of splint was used to bind the hoop. This was a mistake, as the edge gave away in several places. A flat handle was made by running four strips of splint across the middle, from side to side, and winding them with more splint. This made a very flexible handle. The basket is so fragile, it seems a wonder that it stood up under hard usage and has come to rest in the collection. Often such apple-drying

Plate 126. Large apple-drying basket used on the window sill, half out and half indoors.

baskets have been sold at auctions as fish baskets. They may have been so used, but the dark stain of apple juice tells for what purpose this basket served. These driers show a very easy-going method of drying apples, but there is more romance in them than in a dozen factories from whence evaporated apples were shipped. A fish basket is similar to the apple-drying basket but is a foot or more in depth. It was used to carry fish from the beach after they were caught. For this purpose the handle was sturdy, made of hickory and not of splint. Sections throughout the country produce different utensils and equipment for their characteristic occupations. Therein lies a charm and much unwritten history.

CHARCOAL SIEVE

The charcoal sieve is much like the apple-drier in construction. It is shallow, about two feet square, and has a mesh bottom and solid sides. Supports were added to the bottom to give more strength. Another sieve is like a big oblong scoop with sides and a back and handles attached to the sides. The splint is very even and the workmanship perfect. These sieves were used for sifting charcoal, and as the industry was fairly general it is surprising that the sieves are not commonly seen.

Plate 127. Charcoal sieve of splint.

WINNOWING BASKETS

The splint winnowing baskets were made in the shape of a big scoop, with a frame of hickory and with splint filling. Two handles of hickory were set in at the back. The baskets made of splint were more durable than those made of all wood, as the wood splintered and the rim broke away from the bottom. It has been said that winnowing baskets were also used in shucking dried beans and peas. A large splint winnowing basket has recently joined my collection. This is the first one I have found it possible to buy in the ten

Plate 128. At left a winnowing basket of splint in the Farm Museum, or Old Hadley Museum, of Old Hadley, Mass. At right, a winnowing sieve made in a frame, at the Rufus Putnam House in Rutland, Mass.

years of my collecting. It was sold at a clearing-out auction for the large sum of fifty cents! The attention which it attracted after I had purchased it was worth many times that amount. The owner's grandfather had made it and used it. "Where can you find one in such good condition?" Very few splint pieces are to be found in any section; for the reason, I suppose, that any wooden ware made good kindling wood.

Plate 129. Three winnowing sieves in the collection, the upright one showing the "butterfly" fastening.

A curious thing is the eel trap of splint. It was but recently in use as an umbrella holder. The eel found its way into the narrow opening and was trapped at the other

Plate 130. Two views of a rare eel trap of splint, measuring more than two feet long. Center part extends half way down the trap, ending in a point through which the eel cannot return. A letter reads — "It has not been used for at least 100 years."

end in a bag of some sort. The trap is sturdily woven and very ornamental.

The goose basket is yet another invention created as a help when plucking the geese. It is shaped like a large bottle, standing sometimes more than two feet high. The opening at the neck is small and into this the head of the goose was thrust while it was being plucked. The Dutch had large flocks of geese and twice a year, plucking was done, the feathers going into feather beds and pillows. Those soft beds and pillows followed the lean years when corn-shucks, cat-o-nine-tails and oak leaves were used for stuffing.

The winnowing sieves with their mats of splint are works of art. Each man conceived his own way of fastening the splint mat on to the rim, and the illustrations show the intricate manner in which this was done.

The Shakers made innumerable kinds of baskets and many of these were fashioned on a mold. The large utility baskets were made of splint, but reed and rush were commonly used. The Shakers' work is conspicuous for its perfection. A story is told of one Sister who made a large basket in her room. When it was finished it was found to be wider than the door of her room, and there it had to stay.

Splint was used for chair seats, both in the Shaker settlements and in the workshops elsewhere. It is thought that splint was used before rush or cane, but perhaps the matter of precedence will always remain a conjecture. The early splint for chair seats was ash and white oak, while hickory came into use about 1800. The Shakers used hickory entirely. The old splint was made from wood so carefully seasoned that chairs then seated with it are still in use. Today's splint is inferior in comparison.

Plate 130a. Winnower for grain made of all wood and the width of an arm's span. Grain or peas that had been shucked were carried in it to the barn door. Lifting first one knee and then the other, the winnower was juggled and the contents were freed of the chaff or the pods.

CHAPTER ELEVEN
The Beginning of Paint

THE old pantry boxes are most colorful with their coats of paint. There are reds, blues, greens, grays and yellows, and it would seem as if the folk of the yesterdays loved these gay touches to their somber living. An occasional bowl, bucket and mortar was brightened with paint, too.

The Egyptians, 500 years before Christ, discovered the properties in clay for making paint. Three colors of clay were found in the soil — red, yellow and gray. To the powdered clay they added the whites or yolks of the eggs of wild pigeons together with vinegar. They dyed the gray clay with vegetable matter to obtain colors. History tells us these facts through the excavations which brought to light the former life of buried cities, and ancient decorations show what colors were used more than 2000 years ago.

The Indians of North America found colored clay in the soil and they too used it in making their paint. The clay was dried, baked and powdered in stone mortars, cleaned of all foreign substances and mixed with whites of eggs of wild pigeons or wild turkeys. The name of turkey red came from the red wattle of the turkey. If a tribe did not live near any vein of red clay, they discovered that by subjecting the yellow clay to a slow heat the yellow became a red. The gray clay was mixed with vegetable dyes to make the familiar variety of colors used on their bodies, their tepees and their totem poles. They called their clay pits "paint mines." One such pit was located near Augusta, Maine. The Indians' paint brush was a small stick of willow, beaten to a pulp at the end.

The Indians discovered preservative qualities in red clay. They buried their dead in the clay pits or smeared the bodies with a coating of clay. Perhaps this explains why bodies of prehistoric peoples have been found so well preserved.

The white man on the shores of New England and farther south learned how to use this clay for their paint. They called it "bog iron," and red clay was spoken of as red ochre. The Colonists, too, made a variety of colors from the yellow and gray clays by using vegetable dyes. Green came from the crushed berries of dogwood, skunk cabbage, wintergreen, and other shrubs or herbs that produced green. Blue came from the indigo plant, which was imported from India as well as being found growing wild in America. The blossoms of the plant were taken when in full bloom, for at that time the sap was running free and the flowers were of a deeper color. The stems and the blossoms were dried, crushed and steeped and the juice used. Madder came from a plant whose root gave a red color deeper than the natural clay color. Mahogany shades came from the juice made by boiling walnuts, and boiled chestnuts made a buff color. The several shades of gray came from berries and barks of trees; black was obtained by using charcoal. Brown and yellow also came from tree barks — the bark of red oak and hickory.

The early settlers had their own names for these colors. The red was called both Indian red and turkey red, from the association with the Indians. There was pumpkin yellow, so called from the pumpkins that dotted the land at harvest time, and wagon blue, which was the favorite color for wagon wheels. Venetian red is often misapplied to turkey red, but the shades are not alike. Venetian red and vermilion are two paints that were made from mineral substances and not of clay.

The Colonists made their paint in a manner similar to the Indians, and used whey, scalded milk or buttermilk as well as the whites of eggs from native hens. These liquids have an adhesive property which acted as a binder. Later a glue was made from the hoofs of animals, powdered and boiled down to a thick substance. This was called neatsfoot, from "neat," the old name for cattle. In later years the clay was taken from the earth, rolled into foot lengths and baked in kilns especially constructed for that purpose.

A rule of 1828 for making paint reads as follows:

Skimmed milk — 4 lbs. or half gallon
Lime (newly slacked) — 6 ounces
Linseed oil or neatsfoot — 4 ounces or 1 gill
Color — 1½ lbs.

For outsid painting add: — Slacked lime — 2 ounces
Oil — 2 ounces
Turpentine — 2 ounces

This rule was given in the *New England Farmer,* a magazine appearing in 1822 and continuing for a period of twenty-four years.

Houses were seldom painted until the beginning of the nineteenth century. Outside painting was considered osten-tatious. In Salem, in 1804, a man had met with success in his business and one of the things he did was to paint his house. This caused such sneering remarks as "Sam is feeling his oats; he's begun to paint his house." There was no need of painting for the protection of the air-dried woods used in those days, so it was for show that it was done. The custom of painting only the trims of the exteriors or the sides exposed to view was the first step in outside painting. Inside painting began to be the vogue, in the homes of well-to-do families, as early as 1734.

The Colonists, finding that the red paint protected wood, were soon painting the coffins in which they buried their dead. This gave the red an additional name of "coffin red" besides the more common name of turkey red. In the old Granary Burying Ground on Tremont Street in Boston, near

Park Street, parts of coffins have been found when men were excavating which showed the red color, even though they had been in the ground for two hundred years or more.

Streaks of colored clay still may be seen in the soil by the roadside, and often the veins are discovered when digging wells. The colored cliffs at Gay Head on the island of Martha's Vineyard are a beautiful natural spot which attract thousands of visitors in the summer season. One can realize why clay was taken as a foundation for paint when he sees the vivid colorings at Gay Head, due in part to the proximity of the ocean and its forces. The glorious reds, yellows and grays form a picture that artists try to portray on canvas; yet the real beauty can never be caught, whether by sunlight or in times of storm. Indian families still live at Gay Head and can tell many a story of using the colored clays for paint and other purposes.

The manner of baking yellow clay to produce a red came to me first hand. One day I stopped at the country store in Hubbardston, Massachusetts, for refreshments. I chatted with the old storekeeper and casually inquired for an acquaintance who lived not far from the village. The storekeeper remarked that they were digging a new well in their yard and the workmen had struck a vein of yellow clay. He eagerly turned to a small tin can on the counter and said: "This is what I did to some of the clay. I set it on the back of the stove for a couple of days and here it is, turned red. My grandfather used to do that and I watched him. You know they made paint in the old days with this clay, mixed with whites of eggs or skimmed milk."

"I have been hearing about that," I said. "How about whey? Could they ever use that?"

"Yes. But it did not come so handy as skim milk. Not for a big job of painting."

[231]

Today the old red buildings give a touch of beauty to the landscapes. We marvel that the color has lasted all these years until we remember that the old pine boards were air-dried with all the properties left in, and when this penetrating red paint was applied every pore was filled.

Inside walls and floors were painted a gray color. This, too, is a peculiar shade and modern paint does not seem to be able to reproduce it. One coat followed another in those long-ago days and wallpaper was laid one upon another. When hunting for the old pine paneling it is not surprising to have to scrape off eight and even thirteen layers of paper. In one old home, the paneling had been covered with ticking before the paper was put on, making the wall more airproof. To us, however, the beautiful old wood with wavy grain and knots has a charm which no paint or paper should mar.

Plate 131. Little red schoolhouse immortalized by the poem "Mary had a little lamb." Now at the Wayside Inn, Sudbury, Mass., property of Henry Ford.

CHAPTER TWELVE

*The Lyctus Powder-Post Beetle — What It Is and
How to Check It*

IT IS important for all collectors of wooden ware to know
about the Lyctus powder-post beetle. This is a very
small winged beetle which attacks the sap wood of hickory, ash and oak. Its name expresses the fact that as the
beetle works its way in the wood its cuttings are reduced
to powder and thrown out. The powder-post beetle must
not be confused with the termite; they have no similarity
save that they both are found in wood.

I became aware of the powder-post beetle's damage when
I bought a rolling-pin which was riddled with holes. Holes
appeared in other pieces in my collection and I was concerned about my entire collection. A professor at Clark
University suggested that I protect my collection by fumi-
gating it. The entire collection was then taken in small lots
to the roof of the laboratory and there fumigated in tanks
with bichloride of mercury. It was a difficult undertaking
and proved an unfortunate one. A thunderstorm came up
when the tank was open and water spoiled several painted
articles.

I did not realize in the beginning that if there had been
live beetles in my wooden ware I would find fresh accumu-
lations of powder or dust. There being no such evidence
proved that the holes were made by beetles long since gone.

In response to a request for information about the powder-
post beetle, Professor A. I. Bourne, of the Department of
Research Entomology, sent me bulletins of the United States
Department of Agriculture. The bulletin containing information in regard to this beetle is titled *Preventing Damage
by Lyctus Powder-Post Beetle, U. S. Department of Agri-*

culture, Farmer's Bulletin No. 1477. I quote the following paragraphs from it:

Lyctus powder-post beetle causes extensive losses to the seasoned sapwood of hardwood lumber, implement handles, furniture, etc., especially ash, hickory and oak. They work in whitewood or sapwood, especially second growth hickory, ash and oak, which has been stored or piled in one place for two or three years or longer.

The winged adult beetles lay their eggs in the pores of the wood, and the larvæ or grubs which hatch from them burrow through the wood and reduce the fibre to a flour-like powder. The different kinds of Lyctus beetles vary somewhat in their habits and seasonal history, but there is a general similarity. They pass the winter as larvæ in the wood, change to pupæ (the resting stage) in the early spring, and in the late spring and early summer, the adult beetles emerge from the wood and fly about. Under natural out-of-doors conditions the eggs are laid in the pores of the wood soon after activity commences in the spring; but in warm storehouses, sheds and buildings kept dry and warm, the development may take place and the eggs may be deposited much earlier.

Protective Applications and Treatments

Fillers . . . In case of finished products or the more valuable material, any substance which closes the pores of the wood may be effectively applied. For example, paraffin wax, varnish, shellac, lead paints, or other fillers, such as a mixture of resin and lampblack, which will also prevent season checking, effectively close the pores of the wood and prevent the beetles from depositing the eggs which are laid in these pores.

Killing the Insects in the Stock to be Saved

Insecticides . . . There should be given liberal applications of pure kerosene oil or orthodichlorobenzene as a spray or with a saturated brush or mop, or the infested wood should be immersed in vats of kerosene. The only objection to kerosene is the fire risk. Kerosene soon evaporates, however, so that the treated material is not long near the danger point. Neither kerosene nor orthodichlorobenzene affects the subsequent application of shellac or varnish, although in the finishing process it is more difficult to stain kerosene-treated sapwood to match the rest.

In the case of powder-post damage to the timbers, interior woodwork, or furniture in buildings, the infested wood should be drenched with orthodichlorobenzene, a saturated rag or mop being used, or if brushing is impracticable, timbers should be sprayed with this liquid. Several applications may be necessary to determine if it has been successful.

If orthodichlorobenzene is used as a spray, it is advised that the house be opened up, since there is an odor to the chemical which may prove disagreeable in a closed room. Also, in spraying timbers over-head, care should be taken not to let the liquid drip down, since it might slightly burn the face and hands and would be especially inju-rious if it got into the eyes.

As time went on, I became convinced that I had no live beetle in my collection. Then one day the long smoothing board came by mail and when the package was opened, there was much loose sawdust in the wrappings. The board was apparently infested. I turned again to Professor Bourne, leaving the board out-of-doors in the meantime.

I quote the following paragraphs from his letter:

We have found that saturating the wood with turpentine has given excellent results. I would hesitate to recommend the use of bichloride of mercury because of its poisonous nature, although I have heard its use suggested for similar cases (wooden ware). I question very much whether high grade turpentine would cause more staining than kero-sene, and since it is rather volatile, it would be much less objectionable than would a heavy painting or saturation of the wood by a heavy application of kerosene.

The material orthodichlorobenzene which is mentioned in the gov-ernment bulletin is recommended as giving excellent results. This is undoubtedly true on the basis of a number of experiments. However, we have found that turpentine is equally dependable and is more readily available than the material mentioned in the bulletin. Further-more, it is very economical and for that reason, I would strongly advise its use.

As you will note in the bulletin, these insects are a species of very small beetle. They have no relation, therefore, to any of the species of wood-boring moths or termites. I presume any well-seasoned wood might become infested, particularly if there was a great abundance of beetles confined in a comparatively small area. However, all infesta-tions which I have noticed have been either in old buildings or in pieces of furniture, and even in Museums where an infestation has occurred we have never noted the beetles migrating to the woodwork of the building.* The only case of this kind which I have ever seen was where an attempt was made to give the appearance of antiquity to a summer home, in which case the timbers and rafters from an old barn were built into the side walls and roof. These beams were heavily infested when they were taken from the barn and we noted a slight spread of the bettles from these old timbers to some of the new studding which came in contact with them. This, however, was an extraordinary case and was the only instance of the kind which I have ever noted.

*This was in connection with any damage to the woodwork in my Museum.

Following the advice of this letter, I sprayed my smoothing board with turpentine, and although several applications were made, no trace of stain remained.

As was stated in the government bulletin, a coating of one of several preparations could be applied to wooden ware. This is very often done in museums, but most collectors feel that varnish, shellac or wax applied to old pieces detracts from their original charm. The individual pieces of my entire collection are exactly as I gathered them from homes or antique shops, although some of the articles were already stained when I found them.

FINIS

INDEX

Adze, 34, 35
Alden, John, 177
Apples, for butter, 72, 123; cider from, 74; drying baskets, 221; parers, 69, 70; sauce, 72; use of, 69
Ash, 25, 181, 182, 219
Ashes, 108
Ash peel, 89

Barrels, 177
Baskets, 26; apple drying, 221; cheese, 219; clam, 221; egg, 220; splint for, 216*ff;* winnowing, 224
Bath tub, 193
Beds, 56
Beech, 27
Birch, 24; for fire, 89; for brooms, 24, 132
Blacksmith, 39, 44, 46
Bolting cloth, 210
Boxes, first, 1, 161; for bees, 171; butter, 158*f;* cheese, 160; Colonists', 39; drying out, 11; eye stone, 175; laps of, 157-163; making of, 153; meals, 165, 168; molds for, 153-155; nails in, 38; odors in, 11; pill, 174; salt, 166; Shaker, 39, 157; spice, 169; sugar, 165, 168; wood of, 22-30
Bowls, bread, 139; bird's-eye maple, 145; burl, 135, 138; cheese drainer, 139; chopping, 140; eating, 57, 140; grease, 139; Indian, 137; lignum-vitae, 143; milk, 139; salt, 60, 145; Shaker, 143; sugar, 61; tools for making, 34; wash, 140; wood for, 22
Bread, baking of, 89; board, 148; bowl, 139; lintel, 88; meals for, 66, 87, 166; peel, 89; trough, 87
Bricks, 43
Brooms, 24, 132-134
Buckets, grease, 178; handles on, 179; hoops on, 181; making of, 177; piggin, 184; sap carriers, 186; sugar, 179; tools for making, 35, 36; water, 182; well, 187
Bung starter, 36
Burl, 35, 135, 138
Butter, 191-192; box, 158; churns, 188-192; color of, 94; making of, 91-95; molds, 95; paddles, 97; prints, 95; testers, 95
"Butt'ry," 65

Canteens, 197
Chamfer or chamfering knife, 36, 158

Paint, colors in, 229; Egyptian, 228; Indian, 228; Colonial, 229; rule for, 230; use of, 230-232
Peel, ash, 89; bread, 89; pie, 17, 81
Pies, 80; crimper, 80; lifter, 81; peel, 81
Pine, 23, 181
Pine cupboard, 66
Plaster, 41
Plates, 12, 145-147; "pie side," 57
Platters, 147
Pork scraps, 128
Pounder, meat, 78, 119
Pudding, 85, 166
Powder-post beetle, Lyctus, 233-236

Quassia cups and mortar, 151

Red, ochre, 164-165, 229
Rennet, 99
Riddles, 210
Roaster, apple, 47; bird, 47; biscuit, 47
Roasting, meat, 48-50
Rundlets, 195

Salt, 66, 166-168; bowls, 60, 145; boxes, 166
Samp, 85
Sap industry, 104-106, 185-186
Sausage gun, 106
Saw mills, 30
Sawpit, 21
Scoops, kinds of, 73, 89, 92-94, 109, 121; wear on, 12
Scoots, 30
Scorp, scorper, 35
Scotch hands, 97
Scrubbing stick, 110
Shakers, apple industry, 72; apple butter scoop, 73; baskets, 227; boxes, 157; herb industry, 164; pill industry, 174-175; sieves, 209; Society of, 157; splint seats, 227
Shaving horse, 158
Shed chamber, 67
Shingles, 158
Sieves, binder for making, 209; bolting cloth, 210; calfskin, 209; charcoal, 214, 223-224; double-covered, 211; earmarks on, 15; loom for making mats for, 207; winnowing, 15, 212; wire, 210

[241]